Strength of Mind

Strength of Mind

MARK SMITH

Text Mark Smith

Design Grade Design and Adeline Media, London

Copyright © Mark Smith

CONTENTS

DEDICATION

Dedicated to my sons, Ellis and Ethan.

You were my reason to keep fighting, both when fighting for my life and when fighting to pick myself up.

All I have done since my injury is try to be a good role model for you both, to make you as proud of me as I am of you.

You make me smile and laugh everyday, and you are becoming fine young men. Continue to give your best at everything you do and anything is achievable for you in life.

PROLOGUE

3rd July 2011: A date that will be etched firmly into my memory for as long as I'm alive. That was the beginning of the end of my time as a soldier, but it would prove to be the making of some amazing years ahead, as well as times that would almost break me. This book, although a long time coming, has been somewhat therapeutic for me and has brought to the surface so many things I'd forgotten, both positive and negative. I want this narrative to be as open and honest as I can make it, to give you an insight into the experiences that moulded me into the person who went on to achieve things I never thought possible. I want to use it as an opportunity to tell you about people who have inspired me beyond words, what life is like as a Guardsman, what goes on in preparing to step onto a bodybuilding stage, the time that goes into being able to pull trucks with one leg, and trying to play football on a set of crutches.

Throughout my tour of Afghanistan in 2010, my wife Natalie and I had spoken to each other, through letters and over the satellite phone, of our plans to start a family once the tour was out the way. It kept me alert, focused and determined to make our dream a reality. Not long after returning home, it seemed that I was quite effective when it came to getting the job done! Natalie was soon expecting our first child.

This news came just a few months before I was due on my next promotional course – sixteen weeks at the Infantry Battle School in the Brecon Beacons, with the goal of becoming a Lance Sergeant on completion. It would provide us with a better income to raise a family, as well as being another step up in my career, with more responsibility. I relished the chance to run a rifle section in the way I wanted to, having had years of cherry picking the experience of section commanders I thought highly of, and hoping to mould myself into becoming a leader who men respected and wanted to work with. The months leading up to this flew by, as the inevitable nerves of becoming a father and attending the promotional course grew. The importance of both were on my mind constantly, as well as fitting in Trooping the Colour and processing the previous operational tour in Afghanistan that I hadn't long returned from.

For a short period, Natalie and I were a little at loggerheads, as being based in London, and coming to terms with several things that happened in Afghanistan, meant I went out drinking a lot. In fact, I returned to camp the day of Trooping the Colour after a night out, to see the lads queuing up at the armoury to collect their weapons, ready for the parade. I'd had no sleep, my kit was barely done, and I needed a good shower and shave. However, the blokes rallied around me and got my head and kit together, and I made it through the next four hours. It was a hot summer's day in front of the BBC cameras and the Royal Family, with my wife and mother-in-law in the crowd.

Little did I know, it would be the last time I'd take part in that parade.

Having spent six months in Afghanistan and then bounced straight onto Trooping the Colour rehearsals for six weeks, our much-needed post-tour leave was delayed. Finishing the parade meant the start of leave and a chance for my wife and I to get away on holiday. Just before flying, we had our 12-week baby scan and the reality of fatherhood really dawned on me and gave me a clear head going forward. That post-tour leave was brilliant – shopping for cots, buggies, baby clothes, all the things I'd often lay thinking of while I was away. You're probably thinking that's not what you'd expect a tough soldier to be excited about, but I was – becoming a father was very important to me and I took it seriously.

At the 20-week scan, it was even more exciting to hear the news that we were having a little boy. My firstborn would be a son, and I blubbered and choked up with happy tears in that hospital room like never before!

I attended several courses following that period of leave, in preparation for heading to Brecon, which began immediately after New Year's Day. On our first briefing, we were asked if anyone would require time away during the project. I spoke to my instructor and explained that Natalie was nine months pregnant and due to give birth any day now. I was told that would be fine and I could keep my phone on me, given the circumstances, and that I'd be entitled to three days leave once my wife had given birth.

Which I took.

On returning to Aldershot, where the regiment was based, I was told we were flying to Canada the following week and that I, along with the other Lance Sergeants, would be staying on in Canada after our training to work on the ranges for the next regiment. The Company Sergeant Major gave me a couple of days at home to spend with my wife and new son, and then I flew out to Canada. In terms of working within our regiment, the six-week exercise went very well. It was my first taste of working as a section commander and I enjoyed passing on things I had learnt during my time in Brecon. It felt like I had a really positive start and performed the role well, and I got good feedback, both from my platoon commander and those overseeing our training.

And so, the stage was set for the incident that would change my life forever.

This brief prologue is just my way of saying that we're never prepared for the unexpected. My life was proceeding in a way that had its minor ups and downs. It was no different than the life of any other soldier, with its dramas and dreams that seemed so significant at the time.

Mike Tyson once said, "everybody has a plan, until they get punched in the face."

This is when life punched me in the face.

Read on.

1

GROWING UP

I remember hearing a podcast some time ago – it argued that we aren't this present-day version of ourselves from birth. The characteristics we carry and our comfort zone in relation to others isn't all nature, but the result of things that have taken place in our lives which have led us to be the people we became. It might seem like stating the obvious, but it rang very true with how I looked at myself and how I valued myself.

I'd blocked out some of the earlier memories of growing up for many years. It was a time in my life I chose not to recall. Once I left secondary school, I came to realise I could finally be the person I always wanted to be. I found myself looking for the male role models that were sadly absent from my young life, and I felt let down by those who should have stepped up to the plate in my childhood.

So I became a soldier. Joining the army provided me with plenty of people, from all walks of life, who I could aspire to be like.

With hindsight, secondary school probably had a positive effect on me, in a perverse way. This only became apparent to me a couple of years ago – I realise now that some of the situations I found myself in were maybe good rather than bad, because they gave me a stubbornness and determination to prove my worth.

From the age of 12 through to 16, I was 'that guy', the one you'd see being bullied and turn a blind eye. I was the one chased on his way home, the one whose pencil case and schoolwork were sent flying as soon as the teacher left the room. I'd overhear, in the changing rooms before PE, that they were going to break my legs on the football pitch. I'd regularly return home with a torn school uniform and a black eye.

And so, I despised school.

Of this entire book, this is the part I've found hardest to approach. Once I left school, I didn't cross paths with many people who went to Ousedale, as I was away a lot of the time, and I was able to bury what happened. But it's left me feeling ashamed and embarrassed and has, without doubt, contributed to my determination to not back down or be walked on ever since – something that's served me better than anything I learned at school.

The worst of it came one bonfire night. A couple of friends invited me along to watch the fireworks in Olney, and it was as if it had all been planned. Just about everyone who gave me a hard time at school was there waiting, knowing I was coming and would be miles from home. It's embarrassing to sit and write this now, but I was pelted with eggs and chased through the High Street, and they caught me by a bus stop. This is, ironically enough, a place I visit every Remembrance Day, as the War Memorial is located there. Anyway, I'm not sure how many people hit and kicked me that evening, but I was almost numb from the beating. What upset me even more was not understanding why my dad didn't take my side when he came to pick me up. Instead, he spoke to the people bullying me as if it was all a joke and, with them knowing he wouldn't stick up for me, my time at school got even tougher.

I'm not sure why I was singled out for this kind of treatment. My first few weeks at school were fine, I kept my head down and stayed relatively quiet – maybe that was it, maybe I was too quiet. Ousedale was a coming together of educational establishments, so some people already knew each other from the middle schools they'd moved up from. I didn't know anyone.

Why didn't my dad take my side? I suppose you could say he wasn't a very protective parent. I think he found it awkward – being a dad. He preferred to be working away. He always seemed to have a certain tone of disappointment in his voice when he said my name – something that still eats at me now.

I regularly had people trying to cause me injury in the changing rooms, during PE and on the football pitch. Many of them played for Olney Town and, in the week leading up to playing them in a Sunday League match, there were these threats of breaking my legs. Needless to say, I approached that game with trepidation. It was a shocker of a performance by me as I didn't want to receive the ball, and if it did come my way, I hoofed it up field as far away from me as possible. If I tried to run with it, I'd likely be on the receiving end of a dirty tackle. It killed me that school bullying was impacting on my love of football, especially as not many of the team I played for knew what was going on at the school. People who've known me through football since will appreciate that I'm the one who usually went in hard and didn't give an inch – a mentality which stemmed from that one match.

The classroom was a relatively safe place at school – apart from Art. Art was a subject I didn't even want to take, as none of my friends took it as an option, but my mother insisted. She was very pushy and controlling; she didn't want me playing football or making my own choices. But three or four of the group of bullies took Art and, wouldn't you know it, they were all in my class. It was a double lesson, so two hours every Tuesday. It was taken by a teacher who'd set us our work and then disappear out of the classroom for what felt like forever. I'd be sat on my own and, needless to say, my belongings and work would more often than not be ruined.

If you look at any of my school or football team photos, I'm sporting a black eye, a split lip or a chipped tooth in most of them. The one time I fought back, it was in full view of everyone at break time and it ended with me being suspended. I hope never to see the kind of treatment I received at school repeated with my own sons – it's why I got them into kickboxing from a very young age. They should just be able to enjoy that time in their young lives, without having to run on the way home – without the disappointment and embarrassment of walking in through the front door with torn clothes and muddy trousers. I want a better experience for them.

You might be asking, why wasn't something done about it? It's because I had nobody to stand up for me – nobody to take my side. I was outnumbered, and complaining would only have made matters worse. I'm sure plenty of kids went through the same vicious bullying at school – if you're one of them, you'll know what I'm talking about. If you're not, it'll be hard for you to understand.

So, leaving school couldn't come around soon enough. The day I walked out of those gates for the last time, I made myself a promise that I wouldn't let anyone treat me that way again – and I haven't!

My means of escape throughout that time was always football. There wouldn't really be a day when I wasn't playing somewhere, be it at training, indoor football, on the playground, out with mates, or competing in the Sunday League. It was my respite from the constant physical and psychological harassment of school. I loved being on a football pitch, it was where I felt happiest. The players alongside me weren't aware of how things were at school, and the teams I came up against had no idea either, so I felt a foot taller.

I was just a young lad wanting some game time. I was left-footed, which is even more relevant these days, due to it being the only foot I have now! I started training at a club when I was eleven years old. The manager asked where I played.

"Anywhere I'm needed, apart from in goal."

Left back seemed to be the unfashionable position and the majority of the team were right-footed, so I came in at left back. I loved watching players like Stuart Pearce at that time – a proper, wholehearted left back and a proud Englishman. That man wore the England shirt like his life depended on it and it was very much how I wanted to be seen.

I didn't see myself as someone who could be fancy on the ball or someone who'd dictate a game, but I always ensured those alongside me and the parents watching knew I was giving everything. What I lacked in talent, I'd always make up for in effort, something that I've carried with me to this day, regardless of the sport or profession. At that age, I was yet to have my growth spurt, unlike some lads in the league, who were either a lot older than their registration cards suggested or were genuinely shaving while still in middle school.

I stayed with that same club right up until they folded, when I was seventeen. Most clubs struggled with numbers by that age, as teenage blokes, me included, discovered that if you went out early enough, you could get into the bars and nightclubs before the door staff started. We'd come close to being a successful team on a few occasions, reaching cup finals and sitting at the right end of the league, but ultimately, I'd have to wait until I'd lost a leg, gone bald and reached the spritely age of thirty-four before I'd experience the feeling of lifting a champions trophy.

Apart from the memories of youth football, I probably knew from about the age of fourteen that I wanted to join the army. If I could be a soldier, I knew it had to be an infantry soldier. I wasn't looking for a trade to set me up in life, I knew that wasn't for me. The army would be my permanent career, so I didn't need to look past it. I knew that joining the army would take me away from home, away from the people who made me despise going to school every day, and in the army I could prove myself. I could make genuine friends, and I could move out of the family home. So, at a time when most of my peers were knuckling down and studying for their GCSEs, I went the opposite way and didn't care much about the grades I'd get. I had zero interest in a career behind a desk – I couldn't sit still on a chair long enough, and I lacked any real enthusiasm for computers. I was well and truly pinning my future on a career in the military, with no back up plans at all.

But I'll elaborate on that shortly.

A friend of mine from school, also called Mark, who played for the same football team as me, had mentioned he was going to take a trip to the military career's office, and I was keen to tag along. I told my parents and was met with a mixed response. In the weeks that followed, several family friends who'd served were told to speak to me about their time in the military, and I got the sense it was designed to put me off. The conversations were largely based on how they believed I needed to get a trade, but I saw it as someone telling a boy who wanted to be a footballer to become a cricketer instead. I had no desire to fix vehicles full stop, never mind fixing them in the army, or becoming a signaller. In my teenage mind, that was like going to Disney World and only riding the teacups.

My mother was a parent who liked to get her own way. She steered me into doing a National Diploma in Graphic Design, which I hated, but was fortunate insofar as I could draw. Knowing that I'd try to mess up the interview for a place on the college course, she came with me to meet the tutors and, of all thirty-plus potential students, I was the only one to have a parent tagging along. My practical work must have outweighed my lack of interest and I was given a place on a course that, in my eyes, was just delaying me doing what I really wanted to do.

From day one, with the bad experience of school still a fresh memory, I started with a chip on my shoulder – a front to make sure I'd have an easier time at college than I did at school. When others were talking about which university they wanted to go to, I'd talk about becoming an infantry soldier. My desire for that life was heightened by the terrorist attack on the World Trade Centre in New York and the deployments to Afghanistan that followed, which were all over the news.

Early on in my college course, I took my first trip to the Army Careers Office in Milton Keynes. It involved watching VHS videos of various regiments that the recruiting officer was trying to sway me towards, notably the Royal Green Jackets, which was his regiment. It was a process that involved interviews, paperwork and waiting for a date to attend an initial selection course in Lichfield. This would include a medical, some command tasks, a couple of lessons and fitness tests. When it came to the final stage in the recruiting office before selection, I walked in to see a different sergeant at the desk – Sgt Pete Bailey, who wasn't a Royal Green Jacket but a Grenadier Guard, and by the end of that visit to the careers office, I found myself with the Grenadier Guards as my first choice. I'm still not entirely sure how that happened as, funnily enough, the recruitment video for the Guards wasn't to be found anywhere in the office that day.

It was finally happening – the process had started.

Just as I'd had a poor attitude towards school, I undoubtedly lacked enthusiasm for the Graphic Design course I was on. My college tutor, however, was very supportive of my absolute drive and passion to pass the army selection. If I recall rightly, her son was in the forces, and she would regularly ask how the process was going. Coming towards the end of the first year of college, I had in my mind that I'd pass selection and could drop out without completing the second year. But the following few months required a lot of perseverance, as my first selection date to Lichfield involved spending longer on the train than in the barracks.

On arriving, we were shown to our rooms, marched down to lunch and then taken to the medicals. Those who failed their medicals were taken back to the train station. There was a lot of anxious waiting to be called in and, when my turn came, it felt like the longest walk of my life. On being asked if I was currently taking any medication, I replied that I was on a tablet called Roaccutane, as I had a hideous amount of acne. My face looked like a pepperoni pizza, which didn't exactly endear me to the girls. It was also enough for me to fail selection. I needed to be free of the medication for six months before I could apply again. So, my best laid plans went awry and I found myself in the second year of college, but still determined to pass selection and filling all my free time with fitness.

That time couldn't have gone any slower and those I was on my college course with were venturing off for university open days. Selection came around again and I knew if I could get past the medical, I'd put in enough to pass the fitness tests. That selection was, sadly, just as short lived. Nerves seemed to get the better of me and, somehow, I developed a heart murmur – or so they said. Strangely, the majority of lads I was sharing the transport back to the station with had been told the same thing. So, after a referral a few days later, I made my way to a BUPA hospital in Little Aston to have the heart murmur checked out.

There was no heart murmur!

Must have been some kind of ghost in the machine.

September 2002 saw me out running daily, determined to make it third time lucky – I'd added a bit of muscle and I felt really optimistic. Then I go in for a slide tackle playing Sunday League football and the lad's knee lands on my forearm, turning it into something that resembled the hind leg of a dog. Two thoughts went through my mind in that short aftermath: I'd have to come off, which I hated having to do, and would it prevent me from being able to join the army – again?

I was diagnosed with compartment syndrome, cutting off the circulation to my right hand, and was rushed into theatre. I ended up having the arm pinned and missing almost a full football season, as well as putting me back several months when it came to the army. I wasn't able to bend my wrist enough to perform a press up, something I'd have to be able to do if I was to pass the initial selection process. But I persisted, putting all negativity to the back of my mind, trying a little bit more every day to do a press up after having the pins removed. To say this was unpleasant would be an understatement, but it was bearable, and eventually I was ready to head up to Lichfield and make it third time lucky.

It was now March 2003, a couple of years since I first walked into the careers office. This time the medical was straightforward. I was entering unknown territory, and I was pretty excited. A command task followed, which was essentially problem solving, done as a group, to test how well we could work in a team. This wasn't my favourite exercise, as there's always what I'd call a "know it all", who'd take charge and regularly be looking for eye contact with the instructors, determined to be the loudest. They were normally the ones who understood the task the least. I preferred to be the grey man and wait for the dick measuring and shouting to finish before adding my own suggestion.

The tasks would usually involve a few items: planks of wood, barrels, ladders and boxes, and a floor that was supposed to be lava. The whole team had to get themselves and the boxes from point A to point B, in a limited time, without anything or anyone touching the 'lava'. Once that was finished, it was on to a lesson about a practice grenade and, to prove our memory retention, we'd be asked to do a written test on the subject the following morning. Thankfully, my memory at that age was a lot better than it is now, and I managed to recall most of it.

The night was an interesting experience – large rooms full of blokes, none of whom had ever met before, talking mainly about which regiments we had down as our main choice, helping each other to remember what we'd been taught about the grenade and wondering how we'd do on the fitness tests in the morning.

I needed to complete a 1.5 mile run in under 10 minutes 30 seconds to be able to join an infantry regiment, as well as completing physical tests like pullups, press-ups and sit-ups. These all went well, although I was amazed at how quick some of the lads could run. With that out of the way, it was time to get showered and changed into our suits for the final interviews. The time just passed in a relieved blur, and I was told that I'd passed selection. I'm sure passing wasn't based on the tailoring of my suit, or lack thereof, as I looked like a bantamweight boxer wearing a heavyweight's jacket! I'm pretty sure I smiled to myself on that entire train journey home, and I couldn't wait to head to the careers office to finally be given a date for starting the twenty-six-week infantry training in Catterick, North Yorkshire.

I finished my college course and had somehow scraped a pass and gained myself a National Diploma, which I was now convinced I'd never need. I had a holiday and continued to keep my fitness going, as well as making sure I had everything on my packing list prepared, from an iron to boot polish to a sewing kit. Finally, I got my joining date for August 2003 and was then required to attend for the oath of allegiance at Milton Keynes careers office.

I'd kept going and going and hoped that my determination to get to this point had shown my desire to be a soldier. But more than anything else, my drive to make it through that next six months at Catterick was fuelled by a flippant comment made just a matter of days before I'd start basic training.

"You'll be home in a week. You're not good enough to be a soldier."

It was my dad who said that, and it was hurtful to me at the time. He was always kind of pessimistic and negative back then, and I definitely didn't get my positivity from him. I don't know why he said it to me – maybe my army acceptance had piqued some jealousy in him, or maybe he said it to motivate me, to spark a flame in me. But, whether they were intended to do it or not, those words had the effect of helping me kick on in the following few months. There was no way I was going to give him the opportunity to add "I told you so".

I'd just like to add at the end of this first chapter that my father and I are close at this point in our lives. I hope he doesn't take any seeming criticism of him from back then too much to heart. I did say in the short prologue that I want my story to be as open and honest as possible, and that's how it will be. I can't thank my dad enough now for the drive he instilled in me; it has undoubtedly played a huge part in my determination to make him proud, whether that was as a soldier or a Strongman and, along with my wife, it meant the world to have my dad by my bedside in hospital.

2

INFANTRY TRAINING CENTRE, CATTERICK

18th August 2003 was the first time in my 18 years that I'd ever been 'up north'. My family were making the journey from Milton Keynes to Catterick Garrison, with the car full of everything I was expected to bring from the packing list I'd been given. I was once again dressed in my less-than-flattering suit, which looked like something guys got demobbed in after the Great War. It was a nervous journey for me, heightened once we entered Catterick Garrison and were following signs for Helles Barracks, where the Guards, Paras and Gurkhas carried out their twenty-six-week basic training. Those nerves were no doubt shared by the other sixty-plus young lads, all making similar journeys from their hometowns. To be honest, I was shitting myself, but I was also excited. This was something I'd begun to see as a distant dream, having failed to achieve it the first couple of times. Thankfully, the acne that prevented me joining two years previous had now cleared up, and my face no longer looked like a slapped arse.

The first person to greet me outside the accommodation, which looked as inviting as you'd imagine, was someone who would leave a lasting impression on me – Lance Sergeant Ty Bearder, from the 1st Battalion Grenadier Guards. This man had me hanging off his every word from the moment he told my parents to "hurry up and be gone"! I followed him up the stairs, carrying all my possessions, and was shown to the first room in the 'lines', the part of the accommodation that would be for 22 Platoon. It was a five-man room and already a couple of lads stood by their beds. It didn't take long for the ice to be broken – or for one individual to jack it in, within minutes of arriving in fact. I'm pretty sure his only words were "fuck this" and he was gone!

My nerves caused me to laugh at almost anything one of the blokes said. I can't recall his name and he would come off the course a few weeks later, but I remember he was from Warrington and he had a great sense of humour. This, combined with his accent, meant I was often in tears of laughter in that room. Once the full contingent arrived, there were lads from Stoke, Walsall and Birmingham, along with myself and the lad from Warrington. Bad as it was with the Warrington boy, I couldn't understand a word the lad from Walsall said until I got used to his broad patois.

The first couple of days consisted of shaved heads for everyone and trips to the stores to be issued with helmets, boots, uniforms, bergans (large packs, capable of holding over 100lbs of military kit and equipment) – everything that would be needed for the next six months for those who'd pass basic training and go on to their respective regiments. The instructors who'd be taking us from civilians to Guardsmen were four Lance Sergeants: a Coldstream Guard, an Irish Guard, a Grenadier and a Welsh Guard known as FONC (friend of no c**t). It quickly became apparent why he was given that nom-de-plume. If you look up the term "bell-end" in the dictionary, there'll just be a photo of him!

The training team was led by a platoon sergeant from the Welsh Guards and a platoon commander, an officer with a far better education than any of us would-be Guardsmen. We were eased into military life early on – the PT sessions seemed okay, the lessons were informative, the first exercise (working in the field, sleeping out, conducting patrols, attacks, learning how to keep clean and hygienic and cooking rations) was pretty laid back and the drill (marching in unison and as an individual) was all done in stages. But we knew this wasn't going to last, and that was an understatement.

The first six weeks of training were confined to camp, no days off and long hours, but I was quite happy to be away from home and I actually felt like I was making good friends. I was known as "Smudge" from early on, a name that's standard for someone with the surname Smith and one that would stick with me throughout my career, to the point where not many people actually knew my name was Mark. Nicknames could be brutal, so I escaped with a fairly pleasant one in comparison to some, but I'll elaborate on that later.

As for basic training, I felt like I was just coasting along in the middle of the pack, quiet enough so as not to be getting individual beastings from the instructors (press-ups, running to trees in the distance and crawling on the belt buckle seemed to be particular favourites), but not loud enough to be considered one of the gobby ones. That suited me, as it had in school – difference being, it didn't single me out for special attention in the army.

As the intensity of training increased, the numbers began to drop, which, on a kind of selfish level, felt like a morale booster for me – like, I'm still here despite lockers being sent flying during room inspections, or running up hills until the first person throws up, or enjoying a spot of sleep deprivation, or feeling like my lungs couldn't possibly take in enough oxygen to cope with the pace of some tabs (tactical advance to battle: fast paced marches with a minimum of 55lbs on your back, plus your rifle). I always had a voice in the back of my mind, reminding me that I couldn't let my dad be right.

The days merged into one, but we were slowly but surely becoming Guardsmen, through the drill square, through lessons on the various weapons systems, through becoming fitter (both in full kit and in PT kit), through military knowledge tests (both on the history of our respective regiments and on the tactics of an infantry section) and our individual standards were going up, some slower than others. The lessons I least looked forward to were NBC (Nuclear, Biological and Chemical Warfare), notably the confidence test – stepping into a gas chamber in full NBC kit (respirator, gloves, charcoal suit).

No sooner do you step into the gas chamber than "GAS, GAS, GAS" is called by the instructor and you've got 10 seconds to fit your respirator. Working in pairs, you then made sure that the hoods of the suits, lined with charcoal, were sealed over each other's respirators. This was followed by blot, bang, rub – a sequence for applying a powdered substance onto a potentially contaminated area of the body. It would be applied by blotting the powdered sheet onto the skin, then banging it and finally rubbing in. One by one, we then removed the canister from our respirator and, holding our breath, passed it around our bodies before reattaching it, to mimic fitting a fresh canister. But all this was a doddle in comparison to the stage everyone dreaded.

The instructor would light fresh CS gas tablets, more commonly known as tear gas, and we'd remove our respirators and have to state our name, rank and number to the instructor for what seemed like an eternity, inhaling CS gas all the while. What followed was coughing, tears and a desperate panic to be let out of the chamber. The lads who'd been in earlier were sat on the grass, laughing at those just coming out, snot dripping everywhere and standing facing the wind, waiting for the effects to pass. Something that's a lot more amusing to watch than it is to experience!

The exercises became more intense and were an opportunity to implement the tactics we'd been learning in camp and the classrooms. Tactical exercise 2 was the most memorable. It consisted of trench digging and sleep deprivation – lots of sleep deprivation and lots of digging. Each section, made up of 8–12 men, was expected to dig a trench to the depth of the tallest man's height and wide enough to sleep that same section, while also robust enough to be a well-defended position. What followed was hallucinations – for me personally, the hallucination of digging up sausage in batter and chips, along with seeing what I thought was a monster truck in the distance! After days and nights of digging, the rumour that the instructors would gas our positions turned out to be true. CS gas was thrown into our trenches – so it was respirators on along with full kit, bergan, webbing, rifle and helmet, and a nice run to a new position.

It was on one such run that I quickly realised my NBC charcoal-lined trousers weren't tied properly and were soon around my ankles with all of the above-mentioned kit on. The look I was sporting for the moments that followed was far from that of a professional soldier, but it was amusing all the same. There was always the feeling that, as long as you could look around and see someone struggling more than you, you were doing okay. In this instance, I was that bloke providing the rest of the section with the morale boost needed to keep going.

As the training went on, the weekends were occasionally our own, from Friday night to Sunday evening. With basic training not being particularly well-paid, those of us from down south would often stay in camp and venture out on the piss, rather than pay the train fares to get home and have to spend hours travelling. Weekends in Darlington and Newcastle were the activities of choice, although the latter was a much better night. Darlington would be full of lads in basic training from Catterick Garrison and the daughters of high-ranking instructors. It had its fair share of women known simply as hippo-croca-pigs (apologies to any ladies reading this!). Lads would go off with said women and disappear all weekend. Some would return looking dishevelled, with stories of waking up beside ladies who appeared rather different in the morning to how they seemed during the previous night of heavy drinking.

Newcastle was a night out that still gets spoken about at get-togethers some seventeen years later. On one such occasion, a nightclub with a rotating dancefloor and some practical joking led to one of the lads being launched across the floor by the Geordie version of Ronda Rousey. Alex, who drove us there, had far too much to drink and couldn't drive back, so the debacle was followed by a night with five of us crammed into a little Citroen Saxo. It was looking somewhat like the steamed-up carriage from Titanic by the morning.

As the weeks went on and the numbers continued to drop, we started to believe that, if we could avoid any injuries, we should make it to the passing out parade. The numbers had dwindled down from some sixty-plus on day one to barely twenty come the end of the twenty-six weeks. We still had our final exercise to complete in Gare Loch Head – a weeklong exercise bringing together everything we'd learnt in the previous six months. My morale booster throughout this exercise would come in the form of one of the lads I had all the time in the world for – Rob. He wanted to leave training from about week four, but kept being convinced by our instructor to stick with it, and I'm so glad he did. He was a great soldier, and the man could make us all laugh at the drop of a hat.

From the moment we got off the transport for that final exercise, his world began falling apart. I was one behind him in our order of march, so I got to witness it all first-hand and I spent most of that week with tears in my eyes. I'm sure he hated every moment, from his bootlace snapping within the first hour and his boot coming off in the muddy bog, to branches pinging back into his face, getting stuck on fences and the 94mm LAW (light anti-tank weapon) swinging around from his back to hit him in the face. It seemed ironic that this particular weapon was called "light", as it was anything but.

Scotland in early February was an experience, especially for a bloke who, six months prior, had barely ventured further north than Alton Towers. But, as a section, we got through it, and I think we owe a lot of that to Rob. Aside from the light relief Rob single-handedly brought to the section, I think we were all grateful and all well-aware of the impact our instructor had on us – Lance Sergeant Ty Bearder. He'd taken on a group of green blokes from all walks of life, many of us desperate to get away from home and all of us better men for what he had instilled in us.

Come week twenty-six, it was our passing out parade, a day to stand tall and proud in front of our families, and the last day we'd spend together as a platoon before going off to our respective regiments. This was the first time that we'd march out onto a parade square following a band, and it was a moment where the hairs on the back of my neck stood on end. A glance out of the corner of my eye saw the stands were full of our friends and family. This was a day that I'd been hellbent on reaching from the moment I failed my first medical on selection.

We'd seen plenty of platoons pass out during our time in Catterick and now it was our turn, stood in number 2 dress and all with huge grins. I felt like my smile had an element of defiance to it, as I knew I could look my dad in the eyes, as a man and say proudly that I'd done it. In truth, that was on the tip of my tongue from the second the parade finished and we could go over to see our families.

I now felt I was entitled to the respect from him that had been lacking before. For me, it felt as much of an achievement as becoming a Guardsman. Those few little words that he'd said to me the week before training, and maybe didn't even mean or think much of, had echoed around my head for six months, in the cold and the wet. I was glad he put that fire in me, as I'm not sure what my mentality would have been like had I gone off to Catterick with lots of praise and pride. I'd been fuelled by doubt and had a point to prove to all those who'd made my time in secondary school almost unbearable. But I was glad it was the driving force I'd brought into training with me. It had enabled me to stand there alongside all those other Guardsmen, in front of all those families – to stand there with a ferocious pride in my heart that I'd never felt before.

3

19 AND THE WEST END

After a week's leave following our passing out parade, those of us joining the Grenadier Guards from 22 Platoon were making our way to Nijmegen Company, a ceremonial duties outfit based at Wellington Barracks in London. Here, we'd be responsible for guarding Buckingham Palace, St James' Palace, The Tower of London and Windsor Castle, as well as various state visits and, most notably, the Queen's birthday parade, more commonly known as Trooping the Colour. Our first night, we were told by the corporal in waiting that the Company was still on leave and we'd have an extra few days at home. With time getting on, a couple of us decided to get changed into our 'on the piss gear' and head into the West End before going home the next morning.

The night should have ended with a few drinks in Leicester Square, but a detour into Soho was the next stop and young, naïve, fresh-faced Gaz and I ended up in a lap-dancing bar where a mortgage would have been cheaper than a drink. Some venues, as we learnt the hard way, were shafting people for hundreds of pounds, with 'service charges' that were apparently accepted on walking into the place and drinking your first beer. The ladies looked like rather butch men who wouldn't have been out of place in a Strongman competition! It was an eye-opener and an early warning to steer clear of the bars in Soho where the stairs led downwards.

With much lighter wallets after the extra few days' leave, we paraded with Nijmegen Company. Some of the Lance Corporals and Lance Sergeants had been on operational tours to Northern Ireland, but the majority of the Company was made up of lads who'd finished at Catterick within the past six months. We were still, however, the crows (new lads), who'd get all the shit jobs and fast balls (an extra duty at short notice, particularly shit when you caught one on a Friday lunch time and your plans for the weekend evaporated).

Our first full day and we were being fitted with our bearskins and tunics and our names were on the guard list for mounting Queen's Guard the next day. The sequence for the guard mount (Changing of the Guard ceremony) was a complete mystery to us new lads. We needed to pack for a forty-eight-hour guard, including wash kits, cleaning kits for our boots, belts, curb chains, bearskins, bedding, a set of combats, as well as webbing and daysack, including body armour and helmet. This was due to patrols of the grounds being carried out once the ceremonial guard duty finished for the day, and all of our ceremonial kit would be inspected by one of the Lance Corporals at certain times that evening. It was a long night of getting our boots up to standard, which involved hours of bulling (using a cloth and a bit of boot polish in a circular motion to eventually give the boots a mirrored finish) and brassoing every bit of brass visible, along with using a whitener to make sure there were no scuff marks, finger prints or such like on our belts and buff frog's (these carry our bayonets when not attached to the barrel of the rifle).

All of the kit mentioned, aside from what we'd mount guard wearing, was loaded onto a 4-tonne truck and unloaded at the palace that we'd be patrolling once the Changing of the Guard ceremony finished. The morning of a guard mount would always begin with a rehearsal, splitting the men down into those who'd guard St. James' Palace and those who'd guard Buckingham Palace. Those of us who were new to the Company would be posted onto the sentry positions first, during the Changing of the Guard ceremony. We'd have to be called forward to march out and join the Lance Corporals, who'd then march us to our sentry boxes and read us our orders, and we'd replace the off coming guard from, normally, another Guards regiment. The rehearsals gave us the chance to practice all of the above but, knowing the large crowds full of tourists that would gather in front of the fences of both Buckingham Palace and Wellington Barracks, and knowing the other lads on the parade had done this time and time again, it was still nerve wracking.

The guard mount began with an inspection of each guardsman and, depending on who was inspecting us, normally involved being verbally slaughtered in front of the rest of the guard. If three points or more were picked up on an individual, he was deemed as being in 'bad order' and would have a bit of a shitty time on guard, and also when he finished his Queens Guard and was back in camp. Things to be picked up were normally how well-tailored our tunics and tweeds were, the standard of our boots, loose threads, buttons not facing the right way up, parts of our belt not being aligned correctly, whether or not our bearskins had been brushed. In fact, it was pretty hard not to be picked up for something, even a bit of fluff on our backs that we didn't realise was there!

The guard mount was all words of command, exactly the same as the rehearsal in the morning and, as long as we were switched on and listening, it was all pretty straightforward.

The time came to march out the gates of Wellington Barracks and towards Buckingham Palace, following the band playing at full volume which, for the first few times at least, made the hairs on the back of my neck stand on end. You feel like you've arrived, and it's a proud moment, something that you never fully appreciate the importance of until you can no longer carry out ceremonial duties. The significance of that ceremony is one that was definitely not lost on me as I saw people lining the streets in their thousands, from all around the world.

Within minutes of marching through the gates of Buckingham Palace, those first up, the new lads, marched out and were posted by the Lance Corporal of their respective guards. Those mounting St. James' Palace were marched up the Mall at a pace that left the shins feeling on fire. This was to make the changeover as quick as possible, especially in the summer months, when the Lance Corporals were aware that those not first to be posted were left stood still on the forecourt of Buckingham Palace, where shade wasn't something they'd have the luxury of.

My first guard was at St. James' Palace, where there were two posts – number six and number seven. At the time, number six post was public, meaning people in the street could come up and stand for photographs and the two hours would fly by. The other was number seven post, outside Clarence House and facing a brick wall, with no members of the public in sight and where time stood still. The latter is where I found myself!

A forty-eight-hour guard mount consisted of twelve Guardsmen, two Lance Corporals and a Lance Sergeant. The senior Guardsman would oversee the stag roster and which cleaning jobs would be done during the forty-eight hours, as well as being on QRF (the quick reaction force – a group of lads dressed in combats who'd be the first to react should anything like the 7/7 bombings happen, which was the case a year later) – but he wouldn't have to 'stag on' himself. The rest of the Guardsmen would work two hours on sentry, then four hours off sentry back in the accommodation.

In those four hours, we'd be expected to change into combats, get some food and drink down us, carry out any fatigues that the Lance Corporals or Lance Sergeant had set and get our kit back up to an immaculate standard, which it definitely wouldn't be in the summer months, as the sun beating down on a pair of drill boots with no shade melts the polish.

The sentries would finish at last light, as late as 22:00 in the summer months, and the night routine was a bit more laid back, with a patrol of the grounds at last and first light. The accommodation was exactly as it would have looked in the 1960s, and the mattresses on the bunk beds were probably from that decade too. The accommodation was in the grounds of the Palace, but I'm pretty positive it wasn't of the standard for the rest of the palace! We had bunk beds and a small cupboard space for our kit, a cook house, a small gym, a television room, washing facilities that were also unchanged from the 1960s and an office for the Lance Corporals and Lance Sergeants, as well as the storage of our weapons.

When the Changing of the Guard ceremony was complete, we'd go straight in, remove our tunics and bearskins and place our rifles safely away. We then collected our kit from the truck and grabbed our bedding, before heading down to the cook house for lunch. The food was probably the best perk to being on guard, as it was definitely nicer than what could be found in the barracks cook house. A rota was written up for who was on what duty and when – as well as who was responsible for each cleaning job. Aside from that and the occasional shout from one of the higher ranks to make them a drink or to clean their kit (although only some took advantage of their rank in that way, and they were normally the people you'd prefer to avoid being on guard with anyway) it was quite laidback. There would normally be a food run in the evening, when a couple of the junior blokes would take a massive list of takeaway orders and head out to collect the grub.

Aside from whichever palace you were on or who you were on with, each guard was much the same. The longer you were a part of the Company, if you kept your head down, you'd soon start to work your way up to less fatigues. The better, more public posts and the mounts became more like muscle memory, especially during our time in Nijmegen Company, where the role was predominantly ceremonial. The novelty began to fade slightly when we checked the guard lists on the wall to see we were on and off pretty much non-stop for two weeks, which would often mean losing weekends.

When not on duty at one of the palaces, the barracks themselves would need guarding. This didn't require us to be in ceremonial dress, but it did involve standing on the front gate in combats, with our weapon, checking I.D.s of people and vehicles entering camp. PT would be a daily part of routine too, normally first thing in the morning, but in Central London, this wasn't too bad. The rest of the day would vary, from lessons, to weapon cleaning, to range days, to going on exercise in places like Salisbury Plain or the Brecon Beacons.

I loved the lifestyle that came with being based in London, a stone's throw from the West End, so I rarely ventured home on weekends. If I wasn't on guard duty, I'd pick random places to jump on a train to for a night out. One of the most memorable was taking a trip down to Bournemouth, finding a cheap bed and breakfast and heading out. Doddsy and me were that keen to get on the town, we hadn't taken the time to remember where we were staying and ended up passed out on the beach. We woke up dehydrated, hungover and sunburnt, next to a family making a sandcastle. After finding our hotel, we checked out late and headed back to London, mounting Queen's Guard the following morning and trying to keep our ceremonial kit from making too much contact with our sunburns.

As well as regular state visits and Queen's Guards, the Company was also carrying out rehearsals in Pirbright and Chelsea Barracks for Trooping the Colour – a parade made up of over four hundred Guardsmen from across the five Guards regiments, as well as the Household Cavalry and Royal Artillery and the massed bands, carried out on Horse Guards Parade in front of Her Majesty. To be a part of such a prestigious parade was something to be extremely proud of, and the atmosphere on the day was surreal. This was my first.

We were Number 3 guard, consisting of two ranks of thirty-three – sixty-six in total and all sized off in height order, from tallest on the outside of the line, to the shortest in the centre. With only a fist's distance between each Guardsman, an up-close microphone would pick up on a lot of blue air, as lads tried to maintain their line and position for advancing forward. With limited width on the parade square, it didn't leave much room. I was constantly looking to my left and right to ensure I was in line and was counting the paces and steps after each turn. It lasted almost four hours in the middle of June. We couldn't wait to get moving, as the initial hour or so on Horse Guards was a lot of being stood perfectly still – apart from a lad called Dennis being stung by a bee and giving us a few minutes of light relief as it made its way inside his tunic.

Following the troop, we were free to go home for what was left of the weekend, and I had messages from people convinced they'd spotted me on television – although, nine times out of ten, it was definitely someone else. I suppose we all looked alike in parade uniform.

Nijmegen Company was a great place to be, following Catterick. But, although some had settled and were happy carrying out ceremonial duties, and some would spend the majority of their careers there, I'd always wanted to get to Battalion once the troop was out the way – especially as the Battalion was due to deploy to Bosnia on a six-month operational tour. At nineteen years old, it would give me the chance to earn my first medal and see a part of the world that many people who I'd gone to school with might never see. It would mean being away at Christmas and New Year, but that suited me at the time.

There was space for four Guardsmen from Nijmegen Company to go to Battalion and fly out to Bosnia, so I put my name forward to the Company Sergeant Major and, in September 2004, I was on a flight with three others to Banja Luka.

4

FIRST OPERATIONAL TOUR

The flight to Bosnia was fraught with nerves for the four of us heading out together. The Battalion had flown out two weeks before us, so we'd have to settle in at the deep end. Battalion was a place that had been talked about a lot in Nijmegen Company. It was regarded as somewhere to keep your head down, somewhere full of old, horrible bastards, who'd done tours of Northern Ireland, Kosovo and the first Gulf War.

Bosnia in September was warm. We'd been issued plenty of cold weather kit for a winter tour before flying out, but first impressions were that we wouldn't be needing any of it for a while. The Battalion was made up of three rifle companies: The Queen's Company, Number Two Company, the Inkerman Company – then there was Support Company and Headquarter Company. The Queen's Company is the only rifle company in the British Army to be the Sovereign's own, and so the only company to have Her Majesty as their Company Commander, making it the senior company in the regiment and the senior company in the British Army. A prestigious outfit where every man must be a minimum of six feet tall. It was there that I and a couple of the others were hoping to go, but we were told on arriving at Banja Luka Metal Factory, the British Forces Base in Bosnia, that for the tour at least, we'd be joining Number Two Company.

It was as if my face didn't fit from the moment I arrived. Despite being about 10 stone pissed wet through at the time, I was put on 'Fat Club' – extra PT sessions at 06:00 and 18:00, in addition to the Company PT I'd automatically be on. I can't say I enjoyed my first few weeks in Bosnia but knew that, if I kept quiet and did what was asked, I'd soon be able to prove I wasn't a liability. Thankfully, we knew a few lads from Nijmegen that had joined Battalion before us, who helped us settle in. Ty Bearder, our instructor from Catterick, was also in Number Two Company, but I didn't know if that would be a good thing or not!

Being able to drive meant that I was put on a course to drive the Land Rovers. I'd be a driver for the vehicle patrols and operations we'd head out on with our Multiples, as part of the Company. This would give me the opportunity to drive non-military vehicles too. But getting used to driving on the wrong side of the road was a whole new experience – Bosnian roads were an eye-opener in themselves! The patrols were pretty much daily and involved heading out for most of the day and giving us the chance to work with different nationalities, including the Dutch and Italians. On arriving in the areas we'd be patrolling, the drills included house searches, mainly for weapons, but also included setting up vehicle checkpoints to search vehicles randomly at the roadside, for weapons, drugs and human trafficking.

The drives gave me a chance to get to know the lads in the Land Rover, although the drivers would regularly swap which vehicle they were driving. There were good and bad Land Rovers and it paid to sign out a good one. It took a while to settle, but I shared a two-man room with Alex, a lad I'd gone through Catterick and Nijmegen with, and we were both made drivers in our platoons, so we had plenty to talk about in the evenings, once I was back from Fat Club.

Around late October, early November, the weather turned to more what we were expecting – snow, loads of bloody snow, and another learning curve when it came to driving! Snow chains needed to be fitted to the tyres, but the Bosnian roads weren't particularly well looked after, nor were they gritted, so the winter months saw us get bogged down and I had my fair share of spins and hairy moments. The worst was in Bugojno, while driving a Toyota Landcruiser – spinning to the point of hanging off the edge of a cliff and needing a local farmer to tow us back.

The weather was the most challenging part of the winter, and road traffic accidents happened more often than they should. The hairiest part was the thought of veering off the road and into one of the many minefields that occupied Bosnian fields. During a six-month deployment, each soldier was entitled to two weeks R&R (rest and recuperation) back in the UK and, as someone with no children, my leave would be after Christmas and New Year.

Christmas in Bosnia included a 'fun run' on Christmas morning, then a Christmas dinner in the cookhouse. I spent New Year's Eve doing the 22:00-23:59 guard duty on the main gate of the camp, so I started the new year just happy to finish on the main gate and get some sleep. I flew back home on the 11th January 2005 for my R&R, the day before my 20th birthday, and my birthday would be a belated Christmas Day celebration. I spent a large chunk of my two weeks leave catching up with people, and it wasn't until the last night before flying back that I went out for a drink with friends from the football team I'd played for before joining the army. At that point, everything seemed to take a positive turn. Sharing a billet with Alex meant seeing his wall in the room covered in photos of home and watching him disappear down to the phones once a week to call his girlfriend.

I decided I wouldn't mind some of that.

As fate would have it, while out on that last R&R night, I met this amazing girl – a tall, leggy blonde with a cracking figure and a pair of 'big blue eyes' that had my attention all evening. Normally, back home, I was the wingman while one of the other lads got talking to the bit of skirt. But this time, whether it was the lighting in the bar or not, it was me who this girl took a shine to – much to the surprise of my mates, and not without their attempts at cock blocking. We got talking and I was fixated, but I knew I'd have to tell her I was disappearing for the next three months. She told me straight off that she had a little girl called Lucy.

"When I tell blokes that, they usually walk off."

Her name was Natalie and I admired her honesty, although I thought the reason she was talking to me in the first place was because she'd had too many drinks. We swapped numbers and I phoned her in the morning, fully expecting a wrong number tone to be all I heard. To my surprise, she'd actually given me her genuine number and, after talking, we decided that we'd write to each other while I was in Bosnia and I'd phone when I could.

I flew back out with a spring in my step, looking forward to getting to know her and actually having someone to phone. We'd get twenty minutes added to our Paradigm phone cards every Monday, and there was a hut in the base with about ten phones and a couple of computers – for well over 1,000 troops! So, if we weren't out on different operations, it was worth the queuing – when I'd finished Fat Club for the evening.

We seemed to click with our sense of humour from the off, and it felt quaint to be able to write letters to each other. I finally looked forward to when the clerk brought the post, as I'd actually have some for a change. To this day, we've both kept the letters we wrote to each other throughout those three months, and, having someone back home who I was looking forward to returning to meant the rest of the tour flew by.

I'd be getting four weeks post-tour leave, and we planned plenty of days out together. But right at the end of the tour, after handing over our responsibilities to the incoming regiment that would be in Bosnia for the following six months, we had another week to wait around before our flights home. So, a platoon day of taking some old mountain bikes out onto the training area was organised. I'm not sure who maintained them, if at all, but very few of our brakes worked, as I discovered on a steep hill after hearing the sound of a nineteen-stone Fijian Lance Corporal called Joe, yelling that his brakes didn't work. Next thing, his handlebars clipped mine and I was wearing two bikes and the Fijian on my right arm. I knew straight away that my arm was broken – I recognised that numb aching from the times playing Sunday League football. We were quite a distance from camp and my Platoon Sergeant thought I was bluffing it, so it was another couple of hours until we got back to camp. The dark, purple swelling on my elbow meant I went straight to the medical centre, where an X-Ray revealed that my elbow and wrist were fractured. I made my way back to the accommodation in a cast.

In that week, the four of us who'd flown out together to join Number Two Company were told we'd be moving to The Queen's Company, the outfit I'd initially wanted to join at the start of the tour. I had mixed feelings, as I felt like I'd now settled where I was and didn't want to have to do all that again. The Queen's Company was going to be Trooping the Colour that summer, so anyone over six-foot-tall from Number Two Company and the Inkerman Company would be moving as soon as we got back to Victoria Barracks in Windsor.

With a plaster cast on my arm, I reckoned it wouldn't be a great start to our pending love affair, but there were only a few days until post-tour leave and finally getting to spend some time with Natalie. We'd really gotten on well during our phone conversations, and I looked forward to each letter I received. It helped to get all the awkwardness out of the way before our first proper date, as we knew enough about each other to have plenty to talk about.

The day leave started, being a twenty-year-old, testosterone-driven male, I decided I didn't want the plaster cast getting in the way. So, I took to carrying out a bodge job in cutting it off myself. Although the elbow was still a lovely shade of purple and the wrist was as painful as when I broke it on the football pitch a few years earlier, I didn't think a cast would help set the mood.

And so began my post-tour leave and the beginning of something special with Natalie.

Op Oculus/Op Althea, Bosnia, 2004/2005: A young 19/20-year-old me, stood holding a GPMG in front of a Saxon armoured personnel carrier

5

A FASTBALL FOR TELIC

Fast forward on to the day of my 21st birthday – 12th January 2006. Everything had been going great with Natalie. I'd moved in with her and we'd been away on our first holiday together – which by all accounts is reckoned to be a test, and one we seemed to pass. I was enjoying the Queen's Company and it had been a busy time, taking part in my second Queen's Birthday Parade, completing a six-week reconnaissance cadre on Salisbury Plain and representing the Company at the Inter-Company Boxing tournament, as a middleweight. To reach that kind of weight now, I'd probably have to sacrifice the other leg!

I'd been a part of the boxing team for three months and loved every second of it, right up until I got in the ring. That's when the adrenaline got the better of me and I forgot all I'd been taught and had a shit version of an out-of-body experience. On hearing the bell for the end of the first round, I had about as much energy left as a Strongman would at the end of the London Marathon – on zero training. I wish the older, wiser me could go back and give twenty-year-old me a bit of advice – to calm down! But it was a good way to earn the respect of others in the Company.

2006 was meant to be a year where we'd be flying over to Canada for an overseas exercise and, until the day of my 21st birthday, that was still the case. The Battalion was called into the gym for a briefing from the Commanding Officer and Regimental Sergeant Major and rumours were rife that Canada was getting cancelled. I think we walked in looking forward to hearing those words and the brief was indeed that Canada was being cancelled – but that we'd be deploying to Iraq on Op Telic 8 in four months! Normally, you'd know of tour dates some two years prior so, as exciting as it was for us as soldiers, the phone call home was unlikely to be met with the same enthusiasm we all had following the brief.

I had a voicemail from Natalie singing happy birthday. She sounded in a really good mood and I knew I was about to piss on that fire. I told her Canada was cancelled and that we were off to Iraq instead – somewhere that, at the time, was in the news a lot more frequently than Afghanistan. I could hear her crying, but our break to phone home was up, so I couldn't stay on the phone to comfort her. So my 21st was definitely a memorable one, though probably not in the traditional sense.

Normally, with an operational tour, there would be lots of training, briefs, exercises, courses and qualifications that needed to be brought up to date, over the course of around eighteen months. We had to cram all the above into February through April, so it meant not having much time at home. But the closer it got, the more I think the majority of us were looking forward to it.

The worry for the people back home was, without doubt, the fact that it was such a quick turnaround and we were deploying last minute – plus, we had no idea how long we'd be in Iraq. My relationship with Natalie was going great when we did get time together, and I was well and truly in love with her. I think having my kind of job made us savour my time at home, and we filled every moment with memories. I made sure that my will and life insurance was all in place to look after her if the obvious happened, but it was a different feeling than the one I'd experienced flying out to Bosnia. It felt like

I had something special back home now.

The day we flew, Natalie dropped me at the barracks in Aldershot, so she'd have the use of the car while I was away. It was a mixture of emotions – Natalie got herself really worked up and upset, and I just wanted to go into camp before I got upset too. I remember getting out the car and not even looking back. Once I'd got in the gates, I knew if and when I saw Natalie again, I'd have made it back home safely. But, if I didn't, then I knew that, financially at least, she'd be well looked after.

It was a strange feeling getting on that plane at RAF Brize Norton and not knowing when or if I'd be coming home again.

Landing in Shaibah Logistics Base in Basra on a summer tour, we were sure the heat was coming from the engines of the Hercules C-130 aircraft that we'd flown in on. But walking across the runway, it was clear that even though it was the middle of the night, that heat was there to stay. It felt like opening an oven and being hit square in the face by the temperature.

This was Iraq!

A week of briefs, ranges, physical training, acclimatising and sweating – lots of sweating – and we began to know more about what our role would be, but not yet how long we'd be in Iraq for. A group of sixty of the Company would be heading up to Baghdad for the first two months, and I really wanted to be among that sixty. I was happy to see my name on the Orbat (Order of Battle) heading up to Baghdad. Flying up there in a helicopter, looking over the vast deserts, oil fields and architecture, it felt like the soldiering I'd imagined doing when still at college. Throughout my career, I always loved being on the helis, whether it was a Chinook or a Sea King. The smell of the aviation fuel always gave me an elated, complete feeling, although less so on the Lynx that air-lifted me to hospital when I was shot.

The camp in Baghdad was as five-star as you could get for a war-torn country. Air conditioned four-man portacabins, a small cook

house, a gym and a couple of phones for sixty of us. There was a
sheltered area for our 'armoured' vehicles, which, in 2006, consisted
of Snatch vehicles – Land Rovers with enough armour on them to
protect soldiers in Northern Ireland, but like play-doh when it came
to driving over IEDs (roadside bombs) in Iraq. The camp backed onto
the River Tigris, so the air was a bit cooler, just some 45+°C. It meant
that night sentries overlooking the Tigris would be eaten alive by
mosquitos, as I'd find out on the very first night!

We settled into a good routine early on and I honestly enjoyed
being in Baghdad. The sixty men were split into two platoons and
each platoon was split into two Multiples, on a rotation of Patrols 1,
Patrols 2 and Guard. Patrols 1 would be out on vehicle patrol, Patrols
2 would act as a quick reaction force, if needed, but would also get the
chance to have a bit of free time, and Guard would be split into shifts of
six hours on, six hours off. With the camp having six sentry points, an
hour's sentry was done on each post and it dragged, especially 12:00-
18:00 in the Iraqi heat, with body armour and helmet to really keep
you toasty.

As far as patrols go, although there was undoubtedly an element of
risk that came with leaving camp, it was also nice to get out. The city
was, aside from the scars of war, a beautiful place, with so much history
and some of the most amazing architecture. But these weren't sights
you could savour, as the roads, the blocks of flats, the people, all posed
a potential threat – and none more so than the route the majority of
our patrols took us on. They were all vehicle patrols, from dominating
the ground to escorting members of the British Embassy, including a
visit from the Prime Minister at the time, Tony Blair, to reconnaissance.

We'd head out as a Multiple – twelve men split amongst four
Snatch vehicles – and would drive in a 'hard targeting' manoeuvre
on vulnerable roads. Which meant driving from left to right, swaying
alternately with the vehicle in front, making it a near-impossible task
for the men up on top cover to provide fire if needed. I was a driver

in these patrols and, more often than not, I was the Platoon Sergeant's driver. Clint was a man who had the respect of everyone around him and was a pleasure to share patrols with, but being his driver meant we were the first vehicle and, potentially, the first to hit anything or be hit by anything. So it was a tiring task to stay alert to the surroundings and the driving aspect.

The majority of our patrols were at night, and, on the whole, locals were used to the military presence on the roads and would keep the mandatory two hundred metres from the patrol. Although, with only a small British presence in Baghdad, they were far more used to seeing American Humvees on their roads as opposed to Snatches. The patrols were predominantly to the BIAP (Baghdad International Airport) using, at the time, the most heavily IEDed road in the world, known as Route Irish. The arse certainly twitched for the entirety of the time our patrols took us on Route Irish.

If we found ourselves with the Platoon Commander, instead of Clint, we could persuade him to let us stop off at the PX, the American cook house and shops; a surreal place, and one we'd stuff our faces in. The Americans were so well looked after at the BIAP, with a twenty-four-hour cookhouse. We'd often arrive and have breakfast and, unlike the British military base rules on how many slices of bacon we could take at breakfast, these locally-employed workers would pile our plates with food. We'd leave with our map pockets packed full of Gatorade, Mountain Dew and Pop Tarts. The risk that came with going on Route Irish almost seemed worth it for the food at the other end.

We had a good routine up there and were away from the rest of the regiment, which allowed for a relaxed camp. Our CSM was coming towards the end of his career and he treated us like adults in that camp. During our time in Iraq, the FIFA World Cup was taking place in Germany, and England had a great set of players going into the tournament. My blind optimism that came with every England game was, once again, in full swing. I managed to blag my way into working my patrols and guards around the England matches, and I'd even time my phone calls home so that they didn't eat into the football.

I'd been talking with a few of the lads I shared a room with about proposing to Natalie once the tour was over, and I'd written to her parents to ask for their blessing. I received a letter back a week or so later, written by her mum, to say that they were happy for me to ask her. This coincided with England getting through to the knockout stages of the World Cup and playing Ecuador in the second round. We'd been told that someone from BBC News would be coming into camp, as they often had live links to British soldiers in military bases in Iraq and Afghanistan during major tournaments. There was a possibility that some of us might even be interviewed.

I was out on a vehicle patrol that morning and, on getting back to camp, we were talking about me proposing to Natalie. The conversation went the way of the blokes saying they bet I didn't have the bottle to ask her to marry me on live television. Calling their bluff, I said I did, and the Platoon Commander asked what all the talk was about.

"Smudge reckons he's going to propose to his girl on the telly."

The Platoon Commander thought it was brilliant and went straight to the news reporter to tell him. So, it looked like it was happening. Next thing, everyone in the Company knew, and I had to phone Natalie to tell her to watch the news.

We had a room with a few benches and a big screen set up for the football (not all tours were like this!). I had to sit with the CSM and Platoon Sergeants, so they could be on the telly too. Behind the cameraman, I had the rest of the blokes taking the piss as I asked Natalie to marry me. A few minutes later, they had me on a live link to Natalie to find out her answer, so I was either going to be ecstatic or crushed on national television. I was also conscious that the football was about to start – I could already hear the national anthems playing in the background. To my relief and delight, Natalie said "yes", and the moment was recorded by her parents for us to keep. The lads were brilliant, and I was met with cheers as I finished on air. I'm not sure, looking back, that it fully sank in at the time, but it definitely gave us both something to look forward to and even more incentive for me to make it home unscathed.

To top it off, England won the game, and I can confess while writing this, that I know exactly who we played and that David Beckham scored the winner, but I can't remember the date. So, I know we got engaged on the day we beat Ecuador, but I don't know when that was.

As the two months in Baghdad came to a close, another company of Grenadiers, the Inkerman Company, rotated with us and we flew down to Basra. We were deployed to Shaibah Logistics Base, where our role changed and we worked as a complete Company again, guarding the detention centre for convicted Al-Qaeda prisoners. Compared to Baghdad, this was a mundane role – basically working as prison officers. The remainder of the tour seemed drag on, with little sense of purpose or progress; there were no patrols, just guard duty at the prison. It was a safer position, aside from the occasional rocket attack on Shaibah. But, in general, it was Groundhog Day in comparison to Baghdad.

Throughout the tour as a whole, it seemed I'd done well, as I was offered the chance of promotion to Lance Corporal. I turned it down for several reasons – the Company still had some massively experienced lads and some big personalities, and, although I was now twenty-one and had completed tours of Bosnia and Iraq, I still didn't feel experienced enough to take that next step up in responsibility.

I'd given my career a lot of thought during the prison duty and, with a wedding to plan for, I believed the best way to begin married life would be to leave the army altogether. I wrongfully thought I'd be doing the right thing. So, instead of accepting the chance to go on the promotional course, I handed in my termination. It meant that, twelve months from that point, I'd no longer be serving. In truth, I had no idea what I'd do if and when I left, but I wasn't sure my being away for long periods would give Natalie the best of married lives.

The boredom, and that's probably the most accurate word I can use to describe the role at the prison, had played a big part in my thinking at the time, and I wasn't sure if my decision to leave the army was the right thing to do. Instead, I was offered a chance by the Captain to be posted back to Nijmegen Company for some stability, for a chance to organise our wedding and to think over my hasty decision. So, following the end of the tour and some post-tour leave, it was back to London.

Op Telic 8, Iraq, 2006: Stood by the Queen's Company royal crest at the Baghdad Support Unit

Op Telic 8, Iraq, 2006: At the crossed swords in Baghdad, proudly holding the company colour

6

A HURRICANE OF A YEAR IN MORE WAYS THAN ONE

Heading back to Nijmegen was a mixed bag for the first few months. There were some Guardsmen who'd not long passed out of Catterick and they felt they could ask me questions they perhaps wanted to ask NCOs but felt uncomfortable doing so. Then there was the other end – NCOs who wanted to go to Iraq, but missed the tour through being in Nijmegen. Some seemed to hate that I'd been, especially given that the majority of the time at Nijmegen Company was spent doing ceremonial duties and I was stood on parade with the Op Telic medal. But I wasn't there to feel superior to anyone, nor was I asked by those same people just why I was back there. Some soldiers prefer the role of ceremonial duties and are happy to be posted in London, as they may have families or other considerations. For some NCOs, it's a place they'd rather not be, because they're very much 'green' soldiers and want to be away. Both are important roles within the regiment, and both types can be good. Equally, both can be dicks and it was another case of keeping my head down for a bit.

I hoped I could bring something onto training exercises that would help those who hadn't been out of training long. On my own part, it gave me the chance to figure out what my next step would be. It seemed the months were disappearing fast with saving and planning for our wedding, which was now all booked. Trying to find opportunities for work if I left the army was in the back of my mind, and now it felt like a hasty decision. Up to this point, it was the one thing I hadn't discussed with Natalie.

Nijmegen Company had an overseas exercise coming up as well: Exercise Red Stripe, in Jamaica for six weeks of the summer. It was to be, without doubt, one of the best experiences I had in the army, spent with people I'd got to know really well and on an exercise I enjoyed, partly for the right reasons – and partly for the drinking!

That wasn't the case immediately, however. It was downhill from the moment we flew.

For whatever reason, rather than flying from RAF Brize Norton, we were booked on a civilian flight from London Heathrow. It was a morning flight and the organisational aspect of the military meant we were checked in with hours to spare – hours that the CSM naively trusted us to spend sensibly sat around the airport waiting for our flight to appear on screen. Instead, we were in a bar first thing in the morning, drinking heavily, under the false notion that the long flight would pass quicker if we had alcohol in us. What happened instead was we got drunk to the point of flying past the CSM on trolleys to the departure gate, and in so doing, we sealed our fate for punishment once we were in camp in Port Antonio in Jamaica.

The six weeks themselves were great. I learned a lot with regards to surviving using the land, hunting food, using bamboo to make shelters and stretchers for casualties, how to attack enemy positions with FIWAF tactics (fighting in woods and forests) which were slow and meticulous and spent largely on the belt buckle. We were taught how to skin and prepare animals, which plants were dangerous and even which flowers were nature's very own eye drops. It was a great experience, even though it rained horrendously twice a day, almost to the second, then returned to Caribbean heat within minutes. The nights involved little, if any, movement, due to the density of the jungle and how poor visibility was. We lived in a wet and dry routine. Putting on our wet clothes at 06:00 was an unpleasant experience, but putting on dry clothing and getting into our sleeping bags every night was pure bliss. These were inside mosquito nets, otherwise we'd have been lunch for the night life.

Each section had a potential officer working with it, someone due to start officer training at Sandhurst, to give them an insight into the regiment. Our section had one of the nicest men I've met, James, who I'd later call "sir" in Afghanistan when he arrived there to be our new Platoon Commander. The exercise phases tended to be Monday to Friday, returning to camp in Port Antonio at weekends for admin. This was a time to enjoy the small, private beach at the bottom of our camp, clean kit and weapons, phone home and head into the local town. That place was something else! Freaky Fridays was the go-to place – a bar of the exotic variety, with a rotating bed, a dancer wearing very little (and later nothing) as well as the typical nightclub sofas and music. A surreal place that could have blended comfortably into the red-light district of Amsterdam.

The exercise was another good venture overseas, another learning curve and another chance to work with different armed forces – in this case, the Jamaican Defence Force. Just as we were coming close to wrapping up and flying back, we were delayed, due to what the news said was the worst hurricane to hit the Caribbean on record, with the epicentre hovering pretty much right over Port Antonio. So, we were moved to a hotel in Kingston. We were there a few days before the hurricane hit and had the use of all the facilities, including the swimming pool, so we made the most of it and it was more like a lad's holiday than waiting for the reality of a hurricane to hit.

It was an eerie feeling the day it did hit – grey skies, gale force winds and torrential rain. As it developed, wriggly tin from roofs began to fly through the air and telephone pylons folded in half like bent spoons. Whether it was out of nerves or just naivety, our reaction, for a short while at least, was to play a man test – who could stand in the hurricane the longest and be the last to panic. It was something that my soon-to-be wife was less than happy with when it eventually passed and I phoned to tell her I was okay. Windows were shattered, cars had been damaged, as well as the roads, and we headed out in vehicles over the following few days to help with relief work. Despite the front we'd undoubtedly put on during the hurricane, the reality of what we'd been in was evident when driving along the roads of Kingston.

From start to finish, I enjoyed Jamaica, from Freaky Fridays, to learning how to skin a pig, to coming out the other side of a hurricane. It confirmed in my mind that I really didn't want to leave the army and, if anything, it was time to take promotion seriously once I was a married man. This was the career I'd dreamt of during my youth, the thing I'd hung onto throughout those years of being bullied at school, the only thing I wanted to do and what I had gone back to selection time and again to make possible. I'd had my fun and, in truth, lack of responsibility. Now I had to hope Natalie would be able to understand the conflict I was going through and, also, that withdrawing my termination would be accepted – should that be what I would end up doing.

I sat down with Natalie not long after getting back from Jamaica and explained that I initially thought leaving the army was the right thing to do by her when starting married life. It was a conversation we should have had months earlier. She knew I didn't want to leave and she didn't want me to either, as she knew I'd regret it. Thankfully, on my visit into the Company Bunk to see the Nijmegen Commander, he was understanding of me wanting to withdraw my termination and of my reasons why. I took that opportunity to ask if, once I was married, I could go back to Battalion.

I felt a great deal of guilt for missing Op Herrick 6, the deployment that the 1st Battalion were currently on at the time in Afghanistan. The regiment had lost five Grenadiers during that tour and countless others were injured, many losing legs. It was a reality check; the tours of Bosnia and Iraq had been a breeze in comparison to what the lads experienced during that tour, and it would be difficult to settle back in, knowing all they'd been through together. The Battalion had always been a bit of a jolly in the sense that the past few tours hadn't carried the same level of risk to life as this tour and future tours of Afghanistan were likely to include. I needed to be on the next one, to have some understanding.

As a ceremonial company, we'd carried out the five funerals for those Grenadiers killed while on Op Herrick 6, and they were a reminder of all that soldiers leave behind. Seeing the families' grief was heart breaking, yet their pride in their son, husband, father, massively outweighed their loss, and many family members would speak to us at the wakes and tell us how much their loved one enjoyed the job and the life.

After withdrawing my termination, there were just a couple of weeks before our wedding day, and we agreed that we wouldn't take up the option of married quarters once we were married. With Natalie settled in her job and close to her family, it seemed unfair to uproot her, especially as, in the time we'd been together, I'd spent at least a year away from home, and once I went again, it would leave her distant from her family and in a new place.

The wedding was amazing. I couldn't believe how incredible Natalie looked. I let her have the final say on almost all the decisions for the day, my only request was that I'd like to get married in my tunic. The ceremony had two very different sides: Natalie's family filled one half of the church, and my side was almost all Grenadiers.

We'd spoken about children and, over the following few months, the main question people asked was when we'd be starting a family now that we were married. Knowing the Battalion had a tour of Afghanistan coming up again in 2009, I wanted to wait until I'd hopefully made it back safely from there. I was adamant that, if I was to bring children into this world, then I wanted to be around to help raise them.

And so, we settled into married life.

Not much changed with work, and there was an opening to head back to Battalion in early 2008. I went back to The Queen's Company, which was the only place I wanted to be, although I was probably more nervous this time than as a new bloke. I wasn't sure what reception I'd receive having missed Afghanistan, and I worried I'd be seen as a coward. But I was going back a married man, who was now ready to move up the ranks, given the chance.

Jamaica 2007: On Exercise Red Stripe in Jamaica, carrying the light machine gun

13th October 2007: Our wedding day

7

PENGUINS AND PROMOTION

Settling back into Battalion life in Aldershot was strange. I kept my head down for a while, as I was fully aware of the tour the blokes had just returned from. Our regiment had lost five men on Herrick 6 and it was the first tour where it was all-out firefights with the enemy. You didn't have to look far to see the aftermath of such a tour, with people carrying their battle scars. Lost legs and sight were the injuries friends would have to live with long after their time Afghanistan came to an end. I felt a huge amount of guilt for not deploying on that tour and it weighed heavier than ever in those first few weeks back. Friends seemed beaten up, if not physically then mentally, and seeing this made me certain that I'd done the right thing in deciding not to leave the army. The regret I felt would be something I could put to bed once I'd been on the next tour. Had I left, the fact I hadn't served in Afghanistan would always have been hanging over me.

I'd only been away from the Battalion for about eighteen months, so a return to what life is generally like in camp meant I slotted back into the group I generally mingled with before I left. We were also on our way to the Falkland Islands, which would be a good place to hopefully earn myself some positive recognition and, potentially, a corporals course. By now, I was one of the senior Guardsman in the

Company and felt I could take that step up.

With a shortage of Lance Sergeants in the Company, I'd be working as a Section 2IC in the Falklands, a second in command and a role normally meant for Lance Corporals. Better still, I'd be working under one of my best mates, Liam. I couldn't put that guy on any more of a pedestal, both as a soldier and as a man. Tours, exercises and work in general in the military can be dictated by who you serve under, and they didn't come much better than Liam. So I was looking forward to the Falklands, and I knew he'd allow me the chance to have input, something not all section commanders are open to.

We had a great all-round section for that exercise – we all clicked and we all had the same sense of humour. None of us were young whippets, which suited everyone.

The deployment itself was for six weeks, similar to the one in Jamaica – being out on exercise during the week and in camp at weekends, although the weather couldn't have been more different. The terrain, for want of a better word, sucked arse. The ground was like a marshy bog, with 'babies' heads' everywhere. By that, I mean large, solid mounds of ground that meant every other step would be a rolled ankle, and many, if not all, of the enemy positions set up during the exercise were at the top of big bloody hills. It was certainly a place that gave a sense of perspective though, to know that in 1982, soldiers from the Parachute Regiment, the Scots Guards and the Royal Marines covered this same ground under much tougher circumstances.

Weather and terrain aside, the exercise was going smoothly and we had a great platoon. Everyone got on and the tactical aspect was going well too, which meant we could enjoy the weekends more. The Falklands is one of the few British bases to be home to all three services – the Navy, the Air Force and ourselves. The Army maintained a smaller presence on the island, with a single infantry company which, for these six weeks, would be us. Add the NAAFI Bar and alcohol to that mix and it made for some memorable weekends, weekends that normally resulted in our Company's chants of "who are the boyz-a" – a call to arms that any man who has served in the Queen's Company knows the response to: a Spartan-like "who makes the noise-a". It makes you feel a part of something special and, during those six weeks, tended to be followed by 'naked bar' – like, one soldier would shout "naked bar!" and the rest would respond to the call by stripping.

Each infantry company carried out a patrols week, to maintain an on-foot presence around the island – a phase that the locals couldn't have been more helpful with. The Falklanders all owned vast amounts of farming land and spoke with an almost Cornish accent, but they seemed happy to see the patrols still being carried out. These patrols involved each section being dropped off by Sea King helicopters to different locations on the islands, with a week's worth of water, rations and plenty of warm kit. Once that helicopter disappeared, it was just the section to patrol for the next few days – and they were patrols like no other, with penguins often tagging along, something only seen on these islands. Having reached our pickup point at the end of it, the weather took a nasty turn. It meant it might be days before a helicopter could get out to us, so we were kindly offered an empty barn at a local house. Over those few days, the conversations were highly risqué, but they were some of the funniest interactions I had in my ten years serving.

The exercise finished with me being offered a place on the upcoming corporals course, one that I had no hesitation in accepting this time. The pre-course, a week of lessons and PT, was carried out in the last week of our time in the Falklands. While the rest of the lads enjoyed some down time, I'd head back to the accommodation at the end of the day, knackered and soaked, to find the blokes enjoying a nap. But heading on a promotional course straight off the back of an exercise like this was probably the best way to do it, as I felt fit from carrying a fair amount of kit throughout the six weeks. Working as a 2IC during the exercise gave me a good insight into the role that would come if I were to pass the course and become a Lance Corporal.

The course itself lasted six weeks, five in Pirbright and one in Brecon, with HDPRCC (Household Division and Parachute Regiment Combined Courses), a promotional course for Guardsmen and Paras. The course was broken down into a drill phase and a tactics phase. Drill was like being back at Catterick, with a twenty-man room in a shed of a building. Inspections were familiar, with the old favourite of lockers being trashed and thrown, making it hard to keep a straight face. I had a Grenadier called John opposite me, one of the funniest blokes I've met, and we'd just laugh like schoolboys when we saw someone's locker go flying. Such adolescent immaturity almost always led to my locker being demolished too.

This first part of the course was all about learning to teach drill, calling out the words of command and growing in the confidence of taking a lesson from start to finish. The idea was that the drill would be broken down in stages, in order to be able to teach someone who'd never been on a drill square. The object of the first stage was eventually to head up to Catterick as an instructor for new recruits later on in our careers. This was something the Guardsmen on the course definitely took to better than those from the Parachute Regiment.

Following the drill phase, we progressed on to the tactical side, which included classroom work on orders and tactics. There was a lot of PT on the back area of Pirbright, which is a hideous place that I'm sure the devil himself had a hand in creating. There weren't many of these PT sessions where I didn't finish feeling like my insides would shortly be outsides! As it was a combined course, I found myself in a section full of Welsh Guards, including the instructor, with me being the only Grenadier – something that didn't go in my favour. The instructor was a dick of a man and didn't like Grenadiers – he certainly enjoyed beasting this one!

Other than that, everything on the course was constructive and I found myself taking to the role comfortably. Section attack day was on the back area, with numerous attacks and an opportunity for each of us to take an attack as a section commander and as a 2IC. Each attack would finish with a section debrief and a chance to re-bomb ammunition. The day took a turn when the instructor called out Guardsman Smith as the section commander for the next attack, followed by a snigger. Whether it was the adrenaline still high from the previous attack, the culmination of the extra shit jobs throughout the past few weeks on the course, or just that snigger itself, I reacted.

"Why the fuck did you laugh when you gave me the command appointment?"

It was met with no reaction from him, no doubt aware that I'd run out of fucks to give. In my head, I was sure that would be me off the course. But the instructor seemed to just laugh it off and told us to get our kit on to advance.

The attack went well considering, I spent it wondering if I'd fail the course regardless of how I did. But I actually got a distinction, whether that was for speaking up or for the attack itself – in terms of grades, it couldn't have gone any better. Then came the end of the day, sitting cleaning weapons and waiting at the pick-up point for the Bedfords to collect us. I'd just finished cleaning my weapon from the water, the mud and the carbon from firing a full day's ammunition, when the instructor called me over. I knew immediately it wasn't to ask me what my plans for the weekend were.

I had to take a knee and tell the other instructors what I'd said earlier in the day. My punishment was to crawl on my belt buckle through a nice, deep, muddy puddle with my weapon, which was now filthy again, while shouting "Slug! Slug! Slug! I'm a slug, slugging across the floor!" It's an awkward moment when someone is getting beasted – the blokes want to laugh, they want to watch, but they also don't want to end up joining you. So, I did this until the transport arrived, getting onto the Bedford in a gopping state.

Strangely, rather than it ruining the rest of the course for me, it seemed to do the opposite, and I had no more problems with that particular instructor. The final week in Brecon was a culmination of all we'd learned and went heavily towards our final grades. It depended on how well we gave orders and implemented the main responsibilities we'd been taught, which was big on the admin of a section – looking after my men, my weapon, my kit and myself and showing confidence in my leadership.

With so many command appointments to fit into the week, the time went quickly and the course was done. I passed and was now on the first step of the promotional ladder. Not only did this provide more trust and responsibility in my job, it would benefit us financially at home too. Home meant different things to me – there was home with Natalie, which was now my real home. Then there was the home I'd known before joining the army, with my parents. That so-called home was probably the catalyst for a lot of low points in the coming years, long before I'd even lost my leg.

This was where my self-destruct button was scratched away at. I hadn't had a great relationship with either of my parents over the past few years, but I was aware they'd split and I still spoke quite often to my dad. Even though a lot of what my mother had done over the years filled me with embarrassment and shame, I also felt it contributed to the person I was – and not in a good way. Their divorce was messy to say the least – my dad returning home from work to find the locks changed, not able to see my younger sister and forced to sleep on friends' sofas with nothing but the clothes on his back. She hated the fact that he continued to have a relationship with me, and her way of coming between us was to say that she'd tell me their secret. My dad wanted to be the one to break it to me first, so he turned up at ours to talk. At this point, I had no idea why and, later, I'd have no idea why I needed to be dragged into their divorce, simply for point scoring.

My dad, struggling to get the words out, told me that he wasn't my biological father, something I hadn't had an inkling about. He'd met my mother when she was five months pregnant with me, and he said only a small handful of relatives knew who the biological father was, and they'd all passed away. It hit me hard! I had so many questions, but also the answer to the question of why he hadn't stood up for me like I wanted him to when I was younger. My instinct at the time was to reassure him that he would always be my father and that I had more respect for him as a man for raising a child he knew wasn't his. I thanked him for not making me feel any different to my sisters growing up. At the time, I said I didn't need to know who my real father was, and I'm sure my mother was boiling up inside for a short while, because it had just brought my dad and I closer.

But it played on my mind a lot, and my confusion quickly turned to anger – anger as to why I needed to be told at all – anger that I'd been used as a pawn in a divorce, and anger because I didn't need this to interfere with my career, which was on the up after all my efforts. Over the coming days, weeks and months, I was full of questions – questions no one would or could answer. It seemed selfish of them to put that on me, in my mid-twenties, without any detailed information. I began to wonder if I had siblings elsewhere, if my biological father knew I existed. If he did, would he be interested? Was he married, and would finding out about me cause frictions in his relationship with his partner, if he had one? It continued to eat away at me until I had counselling, some ten years later.

I started to phone my dad, wanting more and more answers. I'd always been known as Smudge in Battalion and I wondered what my surname could have been. Why give me a snippet of information, then respond to my growing curiosity like my mother did:

"You have no need and no right to know who he was."

It took over my personal life, trying to piece things together through extended family. I found out that my mother was somewhat 'easy' and would go through several of the firefighters on the night watch in Northolt – but one in particular was married and a lot older. I had people tell me I looked like this or that person. I had them tell me they knew his name and, when I'd ask for it, they'd use it as leverage. I even had friends who were firemen do some digging for me, to see what they could find out. Did I look like anyone in watch photos from 1984? The few I spoke to all denied ever knowing her and refused to give me any more information.

What ate away at me the most was my mother's attitude. This was a huge part of who I was, and those words from her, that I had no right to know as it was her business and nobody else's, really made me angry.

"What's the big deal in wanting to know anyway?"

"I want to know who I am!"

"You know who you are."

"No, I don't!"

It began to make me a snappish, horrible person to be around. The assertion that I had no right to know and it was her business was a nail in the coffin of the fractured relationship with my mother. It will be obvious when I talk about Afghanistan that she had no boundaries when it came to sinking lower.

Let me try, at this point in my story, to be objective about my mother – she was a very controlling person, with a fiery temper and a foul tongue (is that being objective enough?). But seriously, she often fell out with friends and family and I grew up watching her arguing with people. I missed out on relationships with grandparents, cousins, uncles and aunts, because she'd fallen out with all of them, on both sides of the family. She had to be in control, and her callousness towards me grew when I became independent. If I didn't come home from barracks at weekends, she'd turn up in London to moan at me. She wanted her say about which girls I'd be with, and she didn't like Natalie at all. Once I joined the army, she could no longer control me, and I believe that's why we developed a mutual resentment towards each other. To be honest,

I think she may have had mental health problems. But regardless, her behaviour has long since burned any bridges between us.

Of all that was burnt to an irreparable degree, the worst is the absence of any photographs from my childhood, right the way through to my first operational tour in Bosnia – photographs which are irreplaceable, and which I would have loved to have shown my children. Seeing resemblances of myself in my sons and unable to show them, photographs of a young eighteen-year-old me in Catterick, training to become a soldier, photographs from my first operational tour, which seem even more important to me now, given the fact that I will never deploy on another one.

8

AFGHANISTAN

With 2009 gearing towards deployment on Op Herrick 11 in Afghanistan, a lot of time was spent away from home in training. The first part of which was a six-week exercise in Kenya. This would be my first time working overseas as a Lance Corporal and it felt like it would go well. It was hot, bloody hot, most enemy positions seemed to be up massive hills and it involved crawling through a lot of 'bastard bushes' – that's what they were known as, because you'd often finish an attack picking big thorns out of your legs and balls.

It was, as with most exercises, the adventure training and drinking parts that were the good memories. A six-hour coach journey to where we'd be staying for adventure training saw one lad, Steve, empty out his bag that should have been full of kit, but was instead full of as much Tusker, the local Kenyan beer, that we could cram into it. Steve could barely carry it onto the coach and the jingling of the glass bottles was a noise he couldn't hide. Steve had been ushered out of camp the previous night hidden under blankets in a local Kenyan's pick-up truck. We'd all put money into the kitty and off he went. There was a slight feeling in the group that we might never see Steve again and, after a few hours had passed, this began to seem a real possibility. The blokes were just pissed off that they'd given him a load of money – I'm not sure many of us were all that bothered about his safety.

But, like a knight in shining armour, he returned. The next day, every bottle was drunk dry on that coach, so we didn't arrive at adventure training ready to head out white-water rafting, rock climbing and kayaking. However, this was Kenya, and health and safety seemingly wasn't an issue. Within an hour of arriving in the accommodation, we were climbing a 200-foot ladder to bungee jump above the river that backed onto our billet. It was one of the funniest things I've seen in the army, drunk blokes hanging upside down spewing. Some hadn't been entirely honest when asked for their bodyweight before their jump, to allow for adjusting the rope, and one or two were fully submerged in the river!

One lad in particular, Temps, stressed that this was a once in a lifetime thing that he wouldn't do again and he asked Steve to record his big moment for him on his phone. At the moment Temps stepped to the edge of the cage, two hundred feet in the air, and was about to jump, Steve became distracted by what appeared to be a dead dog floating down the river and filmed that on Temps' phone instead. There was a bit of awkwardness when the video was played back – although, to be fair to Steve, you could hear Temps' screaming jump in the background – you just couldn't see it!

Later that evening, hanging upside down on a bungee and being drunk in the Kenyan heat took its toll. But what followed was a great week. Although I enjoyed the added responsibility of being a Lance Corporal in Kenya, one thing I didn't really take to was distancing myself from people who were my friends, but were still Guardsmen. It was something I was pulled to one side for on several occasions, but my outlook on it was that I'd rather have the respect of the men who were willing to follow me than the praise of a hierarchy who could replace me in an instant. I believed that, if I was to be injured on operations, then it would be the Guardsmen who'd have to put their lives at risk to save mine. Would they do that if they didn't want to work with me? Likewise, if I was to distance myself from people who'd been my friends for years, would those in higher positions risk their lives to potentially save mine? The answer to that, in my head, was "no" and that mentality perhaps didn't make me the most popular amongst the hierarchy. But it meant that, if I ever had to ask any Guardsman to do a shit job, I never had to be an NCO who raised his voice.

And so, as with previous tours, the months leading up to deploying flew by and, after missing the previous tour of Afghanistan, I was looking forward to it, although well-aware of the risks. My wife and I had something exciting to see us through this tour, though – the plan to start a family together, should I come back with those vital parts of me intact.

As with any tour, the first few weeks involved getting familiar with the area, the vulnerable points and the locals, and establishing a good base. We'd be operating in the Nad-e-Ali area of Helmand Province, an area that the Welsh Guards had fought hard in before us. The first checkpoint we took over as a Multiple needed a lot of repairing, so sleep deprivation was the dish of the day on the menu for the first few weeks. If you weren't on patrol or on guard, you were filling sandbags.

The Company was split down between four bases: CP North, CP South, CP Tapa Parang and FOB Lashkar Gah, and the initial plan was to rotate monthly. M31A would be our callsign for the duration of the tour and, again, we had a great Multiple of comical personalities who were also great soldiers. We worked well together, and our trump card was Steve! The same Steve I mentioned in Kenya, who left camp under blankets to bring back beer. I loved that man, and it didn't take long before he had me in stitches again. A comical bit of singing led to him having to dig up the ground where a single piss pipe had been used by numerous blokes for months before us and since we took over. The smell, combined with the heat, was like pure ammonia, it was horrendous. I watched him dig up the ground full of piss with bin bags on his legs to protect himself from the damp sand.

Steve was quickly old news though, as one of the lads took a lesson for the new blokes who hadn't used anti-personnel mines before. It was all going well until he stepped on a live claymore, and if it wasn't for a faulty clacker, it would have detonated and blown a significant part of him away. In the true style of dark military humour, his nickname for the remainder of the tour became Clackwork Orange! I've worked with some blokes over the years who've had phenomenal nicknames, but that was definitely up there. To reel off a few – we had "magpie", because he was always nicking shiny stuff in camp. There were some self-explanatory ones: "dog head", "cow head", "welly head", "bucket head" and "cat piss", so I definitely felt like I'd escaped lightly with Smudge.

It was an eventful first few weeks which, for our Multiple in particular, meant we rode our luck on more than one occasion. An area known as Four Strikes was a short distance from Tapa Parang and fell inside our area of operations. It had been named Four Strikes due to four previous IEDs being detonated there previously, and our Multiple would shortly add to that. Sadly, our Company would experience its lowest point at Four Strikes later in the tour. On a routine foot patrol during the day, a local informed us that, during the night, another IED had been laid at this same spot recently. A plan was made to set up a position of overwatch after dark, in the hope of spotting the Taliban and preventing further IEDs being laid.

Our order of march was given by the Platoon Commander and I was told I'd be point man on the patrol, which meant being the first man to clear the route. It was in pitch darkness with just the aid of the night vision goggles to see our way. Not only was the role of point man a dangerous one, it carried with it a weight on the shoulders that eclipsed the kit I carried on my back, knowing the men following me would take the same route, almost step for step. To me, the main worry of setting off an IED was that I'd be the cause of those following getting injured.

I came out of orders with a feeling of apprehension. It was a week before our wedding anniversary, so I used the little time I had to call Natalie using the satellite phone but, with the time difference, she didn't answer. We set off, twelve of us, with me at the front, followed by the Platoon Commander and a lad called Vigs, then the rest of the Multiple and a couple of lads from Support Company who were attached to work with us for the tour.

The Platoon Commander was talking to me constantly on the radio and, to be fair, the route was one we'd taken numerous times before. That extra set of eyes was vital for spotting things I might not – as I followed what seemed like the best route under foot, the extra set of eyes might just spot something untoward on the ground in front of me. We'd only left CP Tapa Parang some twenty minutes and the silence was deafening, aside from the distinct barking of the dogs that roamed free in the area. Many of them had their ears cut off, as they were often used for dog fights by the locals and weren't raised with love in the same way dogs are back home.

We passed an Afghan Police checkpoint. The Police Commander knew we'd be passing his base after last light, the route we'd be taking and the number of men in our patrol. Suddenly, to our left, we were opened up on and ambushed by that very police checkpoint. In the six months we'd spend on that tour, not once were we opened up on with such ferocity and such fire power. With the Platoon Commander knowing it was the police, he was reluctant for us to return fire, and instead was desperately trying to get a radio message through our ops room to the Police Commander for them to stop firing.

We were literally sitting in the open ground, being picked off at will. A small cemetery was a few metres behind Vigs and the lads behind him in the patrol had managed to crawl behind a wall there and use it as cover. The Platoon Commander, Vigs and myself were pinned down, stuck too far out in the open, and any attempt to crawl back to the rest of the Multiple was met with more gunfire – worryingly accurate, with the ground being thrown up in the air no more than half a metre from me. At that point, our instinct was to fire back but, still, the Platoon Commander was positive he could get them to stop shooting. Vigs and I tried to crawl two or three more times, but the ground around us was quickly fired upon again.

At that point, I thought of Natalie and the phone call I never got to make and that sick feeling I had while sat in orders. Somehow, this all bubbled up as a nervous laugh, one that was infectious, as Vigs started giggling with me. We had almost resigned ourselves to the fact that sooner or later, they weren't going to miss. Here we were in Afghanistan, somewhere we'd trained for, somewhere I'd envisaged leading men and killing people like the ones who were firing at us now. Yet here I was, helpless, under the guidance of our Platoon Commander. I couldn't tell you how long we were pinned down, but it felt like an eternity until the QRF (Quick Reaction Force) arrived in their Jackal vehicles and we were able to get the fuck out of there. I can only presume that the message had finally reached the Police Commander, but there was a distinct lack of trust towards them on our part. The relationship with the Afghan Police would be tested further in the weeks to come.

On finally getting back to Tapa Parang and with the overwatch of Four Strikes scrapped for that night, the adrenaline wore off and tears were shed. I stood on the sangar on my guard duty that night, which was manned in pairs, alongside Catling, one of the best soldiers I had the privilege of working with throughout my time as a Grenadier. The more we talked about it, the more I realised how lucky we all were. No one was injured and we all made it back. He told me they could see the three of us lying in the open and the bullets were whizzing millimetres over our heads – I realised that experience, if I let it, could knock my confidence for the duration of the tour, or I could embrace the experience and learn from it.

The puzzling part as to why they missed us with such fire power wouldn't be made clear until we patrolled that area in the daytime and discovered we'd been patrolling in dead ground, just out of clear sight from the police checkpoint. Had we patrolled a metre to our left, more than one of us would undoubtedly have been killed. As for the police, it turned out that several of them were Taliban, which was never a great surprise in Helmand. They had good soldiers and good, genuine, honest policemen, but it was relatively easy for members of the Taliban to influence those men or to become policemen themselves. The men who fired at us fled Nad-e-Ali but, in the weeks to come, we'd be informed of yet more rogue policemen, with more devastating outcomes.

It was soon the end of our stint at Tapa Parang, and the Company rotated through the bases that we occupied. M31A, our Multiple, moved on to Lashkar Gah, although that was cut pretty short. We made our way in convoy, via Mastiff and Ridgeback vehicles, which were built with some of the best armour and had yet to be penetrated by an IED. I was driving the second Mastiff, some ten metres behind the lead vehicle, driven by Steve with Catling and the Platoon Commander. As soon as we reached Four Strikes, that very vehicle hit an IED. Time seemed to come to a standstill, Steve's Mastiff wasn't even visible through the thick cloud of smoke, dust and sand that was thrown up. All that could be seen was a wheel, except it was no longer attached to the Mastiff and was hurtling up into the air.

"Contact IED" was given over the radio and we came to a standstill, awaiting the ambush that often followed strikes of this size. The men on top cover of each vehicle looked into the surrounding compound buildings with their 50 calibre weapons pointing into the distance. As the dust began to settle and the ringing in people's ears started to die down, a thumbs up appeared from the gun turret of that Mastiff, similar to Schwarzenegger at the end of Terminator 2. The back doors opened, and Pricey appeared with a droopy cigarette hanging from his mouth and the valon in hand (a type of metal detector for clearing the ground). He cleared a route back to our vehicle, and thankfully, no follow up ambush came. my Mastiff towed a beaten up, three-wheeled vehicle back to Lashkar Gah. The relief was clear on everyone's faces, but questions had to be raised on avoiding setting patterns with our routes, as Four Strikes had become Five Strikes and would take further toll on our Company, later in the tour.

Being in Lashkar Gah meant an opportunity to shower, eat fresh food that wasn't from a ration pack, phone home, sleep in the luxury of an air-conditioned tent and use the gym. From here, we'd be carrying out vehicle patrols, and we'd been looking forward to our month there, given the incident with the police and the IED to our Mastiff. But it was short lived, as news came through that CP North was up in flames and the lads there would need to be flown to Camp Bastion to be issued with new kit, as the fire had destroyed most of their personal belongings and clothing. As the fire happened at night, many of them were asleep when it started, so when we arrived, most of the blokes were boarding a Chinook in pants, flip flops, body armour and helmet.

And so, that mirage of fresh food and air conditioning was gone. The blokes involved were all fine and seemed glad to get to go to Bastion, for the same reason of fresh food and sleep. What was initially going to be a couple of days became our Multiple staying at CP North for a month. CP North was a good set up; it had a small stream, meaning we could wash. It had a great location to get signal for our satellite phone – on top of the ops room roof, which left you nicely exposed to the Taliban. But it seemed worth it for a phone call home. CP North was located in an area where 99% of patrols resulted in contact with the Taliban, so it was an enjoyable place to be, from a soldier's perspective.

After a couple of months on tour, we were heading to Lashkar Gah, for what was supposed to be our month there. But no sooner had we found a bed space than we were crashed out to an area the Taliban had taken control of towards Shawqat. Moving vehicles in darkness meant the drivers and commanders had to rely heavily on infrared screens, which were a challenge to use on a good road, never mind navigating with streams either side of a dusty track. By the time we got to the area, it was deserted, but we occupied it for the following few days. Some of our blokes took to the top of buildings, others manned the guns on the vehicles or the radio.

During my stag duty on the gun, with a headset on, I began to hear nine liners coming over the radio. Nine liners are a casualty's essentials, from name, type of injury, severity and location. I passed on that someone in the area was taking casualties, as there were several zap numbers (names) being sent over the net, with many of them being categorised as T1 (Most severely injured and an immediate threat to life). A feeling of worry spread amongst the blokes. We could hear gunfire in the distance but, to be honest, that wasn't anything new. We then received a message to stop and search all Afghan police in our area and news started to filter through that a rogue policeman in Shawqat camp had opened fire on several Grenadiers from our headquarters, meaning it was likely to be people we knew and people of higher ranks.

What followed was the news that our Regimental Sergeant Major, whose wife was pregnant back home, had been killed, along with two other Grenadiers, Sgt Matt Telford, a gentle giant of a man, and a young Guardsman, Gdsm Major, as well as two Military Policemen, with countless others injured, including good friends. It hit the regiment hard to lose the Sergeant Major, a man many saw as invincible, and to hear the names of blokes many of us had been working with and had built trust with.

I returned home on R&R in time for Christmas, flying with Jay, who I'd become inseparable from in the Multiple. He couldn't wait to get home, as his partner was due to give birth to his daughter any day. We landed at Brize Norton and there was Natalie, looking incredible with a big beaming grin and running towards me for a long overdue hug. It felt amazing to be home. I hadn't told her any of what we'd been doing on tour, so as to not worry her. Jay was still wandering around looking for his partner, who couldn't be found – it seemed the excitement of Jay coming home had sent her into labour. And so I headed off with Natalie and we went back to a hotel to reacquaint ourselves and for me to freshen up, as I was still dressed in desert combats that were looking a bit worse for wear. We went out for a meal and I found myself just taking in all of my wife's finer details. I'd been convinced during that police contact that I wouldn't make it to R&R, so I was going to savour every second.

After a couple of days, knowing that the Multiple and the Company were still in Afghanistan, I couldn't help but feel like I shouldn't be at home. I was already missing the adrenaline rush that came with the contacts. It was a world away from our quiet little street in Milton Keynes – although I'd soon be full of anger, adrenaline, hurt and all the negative emotions possible, as my mother had one more knife to turn. During my time away, phone calls were few and far between, and with limited minutes, I saved them all for Natalie.

On arriving at my mother's to pick my little sister up for the day, to spend some time with her, my mother told me to wait in the living room. I noticed a framed photo of a Grenadier Guardsman stood where my photo used to stand, except it wasn't me. It was a young lad I didn't recognise. I was quick to question my young sister when she walked into the room.

"Who's in the picture?"

"That's Mum's boyfriend."

"Why is he wearing a Grenadier tunic?"

"He's in your regiment."

He looked barely older than my sister. I was boiling with anger! Why a Grenadier? Why did she have to get with someone from my regiment? Why did she have to interfere with a career I'd worked hard for? This would ruin me in Battalion, if people found out a young

Guardsman was sleeping with my mother.

I thought I could see straight through it – she was having a relationship with another Grenadier to have a hold over me and always know where I was and what I was doing. He wasn't from Milton Keynes, it wasn't coincidence – she'd met him intentionally, to hurt me, knowing that through him she could keep tabs on the regiment. I could see she was using him, and I'd be proven right a couple of years down the line.

He was eighteen and she was in her fifties, for fuck's sake!

He was actually hiding in the garage when I came round for my sister, and my mother's response to my anger was that I was being paranoid – that no one would care if they knew in Battalion. She was loving how annoyed I was. Her scheme had worked – not only did she relish the fact that I now knew my dad wasn't my biological father and that she was the only one who knew who the real one was, now she was interfering with my career in the worst way possible.

I flew back out to Afghanistan at the end of my R&R and spoke to a couple of close friends who I could trust and also to the Platoon Commander. We were aware some new lads would be flying out to join us soon, and I wanted to ensure that this particular lad wouldn't be one of them – for the benefit of both of us. I was reassured that he wasn't, and the tour cracked on for me.

Our Company had its first major casualty of the tour soon afterwards and the aftermath changed our objectives. Mr Banks, one of the Platoon Commanders, was injured after setting off an IED on entering a compound, losing both legs and part of a hand as a result. Mr Banks and our Platoon Commander were good friends and it led to our PC taking over from him and us having a new PC. Our new guy was the same officer I'd worked with in Jamaica a few years previous. It was brilliant to see that he'd made it and had chosen the Grenadiers, and I was happy to get the opportunity to work with him again. I consider myself very lucky that I had the privilege to work under two of the

Battalion's best officers during Afghanistan. Both were on a level that enabled us to have a real positive input on the Multiple.

It was fighting season in Nad-e-Ali and it became almost addictive. I hated patrols where we carried heavy kit for hours on end without a fight. I wasn't really the trusting sort and much preferred the simplicity of knowing who the enemy was and having a good scrap. We would, as a Multiple, spend the remainder of the tour away from Lashkar Gah, and through CP North and CP South we'd have plenty of opportunities to experience that euphoria. I'm sure people outside the military struggle to understand how you can possibly enjoy the high that comes from the near misses and struggle further to understand how, in those moments, we're often found laughing. I think it was a nervous reaction on my part, and also a way to lighten the mood around me. I thought if the other, younger lads could see me smiling in times of uncertainty, they too would grow in confidence.

That attitude saw me through probably the funniest, yet closest contact we had on that tour. We'd moved out on a fighting patrol, to push the FLET (Forward Line of Enemy Troops), to dominate the ground and reassure the locals that we were forcing the Taliban out of the area. During patrols when you pushed into an area like this, the atmosphere tended to be the earliest warning sign that Taliban were close. There would be no farmers, no children, no cars, just a silence. It was pouring down with rain and the routes we took meant our boots were heavy with mud, and the grind of pushing through streams to avoid vulnerable areas with potential IEDs meant everyone was hoping this would all be worth it.

We pushed out further than we had all tour and went firm, when a Taliban fighter with an AK47 popped up over a wall no more than ten metres away and fired. Jay, being point man, was furthest from cover and needed to peel left to get into better cover. But the wet ground meant he Klinsmann-like (football analogy) dived on his belly towards my feet, covered in mud with his Light Machine Gun in hand, and I found it hilarious. What followed was bonfire night-level of fire from both parties and that unmistakeable crack and thump sound of bullets coming close to hitting. We had a small team of Americans attached to us to call in air strikes, and I'm sure they thought we were on day release from the nuthouse. That day was one of the highest we had, and we felt like we'd gone in some small way to pushing the Taliban back for Mr Banks, as this was within the area of the compound where he'd been injured.

As with that particular fighting patrol, I often found a way to take in the funny moments as well as the gravity of the role, and in hindsight, I'm glad I did. After that initial contact of coming under fire from the Afghan Police, I adopted a mindset of finding ways to laugh during shit times, depending on the circumstances. We were all well aware that our card could be stamped at any moment, so I wanted to be able to look at myself in a mirror if the time came and know that, under tough situations, I was able to clear my head enough to be fully in that moment – not worried about what I stood to lose back home if anything happened. I didn't want to look in that metaphorical mirror and know I was a liability to my friends. Though I didn't know it at the time, that ability to laugh in dangerous times would unknowingly go on to help me come to terms with becoming an amputee.

I found humour on most operations we did. It normally involved people flapping to get a weapon prepped under pressure or people diving for cover into deep streams, as was the case in Babaji, during the biggest operation to happen in Helmand Province at that time – Op Moshtarak. To be honest, I could write all day about the good memories from my time there, and I couldn't have shared that experience in better company. Those reading this who were part of M31A will know the moments we've been lucky to share together over a beer since – thankfully, all still here. When we get together, the good memories outweigh the bad; it tends to be in times of quiet and solitude that we acknowledge the not-so-good times. That rang true for the Company towards the end of the tour, as we began to get that glimmer of looking forward to being home and trying to remember what normality was.

I said, during our Multiple's IED strike on the Mastiff at Four Strikes, that sometimes people higher up, not being out on the ground every day, become desensitised to the risks of pattern setting. The Taliban, to their credit, use the land, the compounds and what they can make firmly to their advantage. That farmer you notice stopping his work to watch your patrol, those children you see running towards their village on spotting you, they watch you too, looking for weaknesses and patterns. Sadly, our Company used Four Strikes on numerous occasions to safely mark out a route for convoys to pass through.

I kept a diary in Afghanistan, the first time I'd done so anywhere I'd been. It was because I'd already decided I wouldn't tell Natalie any of what was going on while we were away, but she could read it all at the end of the tour, knowing I was safely home. I wrote in it every day, right up until six weeks before the end of the tour, when our platoon's other Multiple had been tasked to secure Four Strikes for our Multiple to come through in vehicles. The same spot that had caused such damage to Steve's Mastiff caused far worse to a much less armoured Jackal vehicle, costing the life of LSgt Dave Greenhalgh and injuring three others from our Company.

Dave was someone I respected a lot as a soldier. The army was his life, he loved being a Grenadier – a very proud, loud, hardworking man and a natural leader. I'm not sure we ever quite saw eye to eye on how we did things and it would be disrespectful to his memory to say otherwise, but he left a big hole in the Company and a big hole in friends of mine who were really close to him. Arriving at the area, I met with a scene and smell that will always stick with me. Dave and the other lads who'd been injured had already been flown to Bastion and we were tasked with what was left.

It was a numb way to finish the tour.

2009: Our pre-deployment photographs taken before Herrick 11 in Afghanistan

Op Herrick 11, Afghanistan, 2009–2010: Our multiple, M31A, with our WMIK Vehicles before heading out on patrol in Nad-e-Ali (I'm in the driver's seat, centre vehicle)

Op Herrick 11, Afghanistan, 2009–2010: On patrol with the Afghan National Army

9

THE END OF MY CAREER

've always loved playing football. I'd play seven days a week when I was growing up if I could. I was lucky that I got to continue playing in the army and was proud to represent the regiment on several occasions. I can still vividly remember the last time I ever got to play football with two legs, and it was in Battalion, playing in the Manchester Cup for the Queen's Company in the inter-company football tournament at Wellington Barracks in London. Had I known that would be the last time I'd play able-bodied, I wouldn't have stopped. It was also the last time I'd take part in Trooping the Colour, and it seemed a good way to bow out, with the Queen's Company escorting the colour in 2010, which was to be my fourth Queen's birthday parade.

It was a busy time following on from Afghanistan and it flew by for two reasons – Natalie was pregnant and expecting our first child, and I would soon be heading on my next promotional course, the Section Commanders battle course: sixteen weeks in the Brecon Beacons. I was determined to pass the course, to take that next step in my career and become a Lance Sergeant. Making that step up from a section 2IC to a section commander would provide more financial security for our growing family. I couldn't wait to become a dad, we'd talked about parenthood since we'd got married, but I'd known I wanted to get Afghanistan out of the way first. Making it to the end of that tour, with how it finished, losing Dave, I felt very lucky and fortunate that our Multiple made it through. To step onto the Chinook, knowing we'd shortly be on our way home, was a moment of relief and also the first time my heart fluttered a little – we could actually start a family now. Little did I know that being around to raise a family wasn't to be a given, even with that tour finished.

One of my last nights with the Queen's Company before heading off to Brecon also coincided with one of my good mates, Steve, leaving the army. So, what better way to see him off than a flat party – flat parties were a common occurrence in the Company. A car full of alcohol had been collected earlier in the day, including one loud stereo, a corridor for Crow Olympics (an initiation ceremony of sorts, involving drinking, joking, drunken races and other unmentionable shenanigans) and well over fifty blokes squeezed into an area meant for a couple of people. That flat party was one that's still talked about now – bedding and beds being thrown from windows, naked wrestling, empty beer bottles lined up like pins in bowling and Jay and myself picking blokes up who were wearing nothing but a weightlifting belt, as they were thrown and slid into the empty bottles.

It's times like those that I miss, even now. The lifestyle of being a soldier carried with it risk, time away from home, aches, pains and sleep deprivation. But those moments of hardship were often buried and forgotten by memories of nights like that – memories that bring tears of laughter to the eyes. Realising those moments are gone is sad, but I think for those of us who are no longer serving, there's an expectation to grow up and be responsible outside of the army. I mean, nakedness at parties is largely frowned upon in civvy street, and that was hard to take and adjust to for some time. It was almost like grieving for a part of me that got left behind.

Just like my leg!

The next morning, it looked like a zombie apocalypse had

struck: blokes as pale and grey as Brecon's skies were over the next few months and the floor barely visible through the sea of empty bottles, along with the odd bloke who hadn't quite made it back to his room and had instead given up hope and slept in the corridor. I disappeared on leave before starting my course and hoped I'd be returning to join those mates as a Lance Sergeant and also a dad.

My course started the day after New Year's Day and, with Natalie almost nine months pregnant, it was a quiet one, which was what I needed before the drive to Brecon. Courses like this bring you together with men from all infantry regiments; there'd be a few from your own, but you'd barely see each other. They were a mix and match, with the arselickers quickly standing out, the blokes who were there because they were phenomenally fit, the blokes who'd been in for years and the grey men. My mindset on any course like this was to be the grey man for as long as possible, to get to figure people out – who would stab you in the back in order to be seen to be a switched-on bloke in front of the instructors, who were the funny ones and who were genuinely good, all-round soldiers. I tried to slot myself somewhere around there, although I was well aware that, when it came to the fitness tests, I'd be hovering around the mid to lower third of the course. Military fitness is a concept of one size fits all, and many good soldiers have been overlooked or written off because they can't run 1.5 miles in under 9 minutes yet, tactically, are some of the best soldiers there are.

I knew my classroom-based work had to be on the ball to give me a chance of getting a good grade on this course, and my evenings and weekends would be spent writing orders, lesson plans, safety plans and all that good stuff. I knew if I put the detail into those areas, it would serve me well. The grades I was getting for the confidence in the delivery of my lessons and my written work were better than what I could have hoped for and I was fortunate to be in a really good section, where the blokes were squaring each other away in prompts and hints when needed in the delivery of their own lessons.

I felt well prepared in terms of experience to be on this course, with three operational tours under my belt and, at twenty-six years old, I was one of the older blokes in the section. So I felt confident in the delivery and understanding of the role of a Section Commander and as an instructor, but the fitness side of things still makes me feel sick now! The course was broken down into two eight-week periods. The first phase was skill at arms, training us to become instructors on every weapon system an infantryman would use, as well as training us to become qualified in overseeing and running live firing ranges (shooting scenarios involving live ammunition and wooden or metal targets, with various encompassments, distances and numbers of soldiers taking part), a qualification that would be almost the death of me some six months later.

Each lesson would have to be learnt to the letter and taught by us, word for word, with enthusiasm, confidence and an understanding of what we were teaching. At that time, I had a good memory and picked up the lesson plans and terminology well, and I was getting good grades in the delivery of results. The weekends were often free, at least in terms of being at home, but the long drive from Brecon to Milton Keynes and back took up a fair bit of time, as did the 'homework' each weekend, writing reports and lesson plans.

On Friday 21st January 2011, after a long trip home and a long week on the course, I drove down our street to see the mother-in-law's car outside our house. On walking in, I noticed that Natalie looked a bit red-faced and in some discomfort – she was having contractions every few minutes! She gave birth the following morning at 09:21 to Ellis Mark Smith, weighing 7lb 14oz, and I cried my eyes out. I went outside to phone my instructor and was told that the Sergeant Major said I couldn't use the three days leave, as I'd miss too much and would lose my place on the Section Commanders battle course. I'd have to return as normal the following day. I went back in to tell Natalie and

I said I'd come off the course – another one would come up at some point. I just wanted to spend every second I had with this little man. Natalie talked me round with some words of wisdom, as she often has. The next day, I was heading back to Brecon, with some tears in my eyes after laying Ellis down in his cot, and with a determination to see the course out and make the time away worthwhile.

It broke my heart every Sunday evening to set off back to Brecon and not be able to see Ellis. Just being away for the week, I'd come home to so many changes in what he could do. The time at home wasn't even quality time, as I'd have coursework that would need writing up ready for the following week and so the Saturdays were largely spent shut away writing. The job certainly required the patience of a good woman – the time spent away, the last-minute changes of plan, my not being around to help with the night feeds and all the things expected of a husband and father, were harder for Natalie than they were for me. Despite parts of my course involving sleep deprivation, it was Natalie who looked like she could do with a long holiday.

The weeks felt like they were going backwards, and the completion of the skill at arms phase, after week eight, meant I was now qualified to teach soldiers on various weapons systems, as well as being a qualified range safety supervisor. The conclusion of the skill at arms phase signalled the start of the next eight weeks – tactics. Tactics meant different instructors, different lessons, a lot more physicality, a lot less sleep and a lot more time spent on attacks, ambushes, reconnaissance patrols and all the bread-and-butter of becoming a Section Commander, capable of leading a group of men into battle. Physically, I hung out of my arse every single day. I knew I could excel tactically and in terms of soldiering and writing orders and such like, but physically, the front of the pack was a mirage!

My outlook was that if I could lead men who understood what I asked of them and I could execute that role well, then I could be a good Section Commander. I knew from Afghanistan that adrenaline can play an amazing part in just how fast a man can run with his own bodyweight on his back when being shot at, so I felt that it was more important to have a grasp of tactics – as opposed to being that man at the front of all the timed runs and fitness tests, but not having a clue when it came to really understanding the role. I felt the longer the course went on and the more we all clicked and learnt each others' strengths and weaknesses, the more my confidence grew, and so, the sixteen weeks came to a close and I passed the course. I came away from it with a B+ grade, which I was really happy with, and returned to my regiment to be promoted.

Returning back to the Battalion would now mean promotion to a Lance Sergeant and taking over my own section. I'd quickly get the opportunity to put all I'd learnt in Brecon, and what I'd taken on board from good leaders over the years, into practice. The Company was off to Canada on Exercise Prairie Storm, a pre-deployment exercise much like the trip to Kenya before the previous tour of Afghanistan. Having recently been promoted, this also meant I was now qualified to work as staff on live firing ranges, and so not only would I be on exercise with the Company for six weeks, I'd also be staying in Canada to help with the ranges for the regiment after us, which meant I still wouldn't be spending much time at home with my new-born son.

The exercise went well, and I enjoyed the added responsibility and the fact that extra chevron on my rank slide meant that my ideas were listened to more now. The downside, though, was the lack of communication back home; I relied on letters to keep up with Natalie and Ellis.

That extra chevron didn't feel like a weight when it came to working in the field, I felt like I thrived in the role. But in camp it was something I would, at times, rather not have had. I was pulled to one side more than once, as it was noticed that I hadn't really settled into the customs that came with being in the Sergeant's Mess. Déjà vu from when I became a Lance Corporal previously. I had good friends who were still Guardsmen and, although I had added responsibility now, I wasn't going to cut those ties with friends of mine. The good friends understood I had a slightly different role now, but remaining close to them meant that they also understood that, at times, I'd have to ask them to help out with the shit jobs. Staying loyal, which was something I prided myself on as a person, meant they'd work hard for me.

Following the completion of our exercise, it was time for those of us who were qualified to join the permanent safety staff, who'd be overseeing the live firing of the Yorkshire Regiment. The permanent safety staff were lads from all different regiments posted to Canada for two years to oversee the safety of the same ranges every six weeks. Some of these lads had been the safety for our regiment during our exercise and seemed impressed with a lot of our tactics, techniques and procedures. We had, however, clashed with several of them in a bar a few nights previously, so working alongside them had the potential to be interesting. Along with the permanent staff, they knew the ranges inside out and so, going through them over and over again was something like Groundhog Day to them.

After a few days of classroom briefs, the temporary safety staff, consisting partly of those of us from the Grenadier Guards, were split up to work with different teams. At first, I was due to work alongside some of the blokes from the Grenadiers, going through the same ranges we'd gone through ourselves during our exercise – which I was quite happy with. Then the chance came up to work with the armoured infantry staff on very different ranges, ranges we hadn't gone through before, which involved very different attacks and tactics to those we were used to. But it meant six weeks of moving everywhere on the back of vehicles and not on foot which, after our exercise, seemed the easy option.

I hopped in a wagon with another safety staff member to join the team we'd be working with, who were already out on the ranges repairing the sandbags, walls and targets from the previous exercise.

I jumped off the vehicle to see the majority of the lads were the same ones we'd had a run in with in the pub a few days prior. A little awkward "hello", followed by a couple of days of shit taskings, and it was fine. They were good blokes, and I was keen to pick their brains to get me up to speed with the layout of the armoured infantry ranges and how the tactics would differ to the ones we'd been using.

I asked a lot of questions and, for the most part, got helpful answers. The only one who seemed deliberately was the range conducting officer himself, a Major from the Rifles, an arrogant arsehole of a man. Every question was a nuisance to him, despite the ranges being orchestrated by him. Thankfully, those who'd had the dubious pleasure of working under him for several months already were aware he could do with some people skills. The live firing ranges began in the following days. As with any ranges involving live ammunition, the numbers start smaller, with ticks in the boxes to ensure every soldier is competent to progress onto the larger scale attacks.

And so, 3rd July 2011 came around.

An early start, before first light, and several range vehicles set off from the pick-up point earlier than the time stated. I had to jump into the last one with the aforementioned arsehole officer. I think I'd sooner have jumped in an Uber with one of the blokes from my time at secondary school than with him. On the drive out to the range, I sent my wife a quick text. Given the time difference, I knew she wouldn't see it for a few hours but, as I sent it, I remember having the same eerie feeling that I used to get before patrols in Afghanistan – patrols that normally resulted in shit hitting the fan.

The range day consisted of a platoon attack. Platoon attacks consist of around thirty soldiers, operating in three sections, and it requires a lot of control and understanding to keep them running as smoothly as possible. The layout started with the soldiers mounted in the back of Warrior armoured vehicles, using their 30mm cannon to fire at the first position. The soldiers would then disembark from the rear, clearing a bunker position on foot, through a hideous boggy marsh. As safety staff, we were dressed in high visibility vests to separate ourselves, and their disembarking from the armoured vehicles was our cue to follow.

Moving on, once the soldiers advanced, it brought them onto a trench system, where there were several enemy positions to clear. Our role, as well as ensuring they were carrying out their drills safely, was to test their casualty evacuation drills. Any soldiers who weren't necessarily making good use of cover received a tap on the shoulder to be told they'd been shot, and it was then down to the commanders amongst them to ensure the casualties were evacuated back to a safe location on the range to receive medical treatment. Once all trench positions were cleared, the final part of the range was an advance onto three compounds – small buildings similar to those to be searched or cleared in Afghanistan but, in this instance, built of light MDF wood.

The section I was following for the first platoon attack stayed in the trenches to provide fire support and didn't advance to the compounds. On clearing all three compounds, "STOP! STOP! STOP!", was called by the safety staff and this signalled the conclusion of the range. Safety catches were applied and, under the direction of the safety staff, the weapons were unloaded in a safe direction and the soldiers made their way back to the admin point at the start for a debrief on how the range was carried out.

There were a few concerns on safety angles, communication problems via radios – notably the fact that a shortage of radios meant temporary staff, such as myself, didn't have one at all, and that led to an element of disorientation. Once again, I was met with a comment of "just get on with it" from the range conducting officer. The fact of the matter was, it was unsafe for me to be on this range without the relevant equipment, and it went against the standing orders for the range. But, as a newly promoted Lance Sergeant and on my first external work (working with other regiments), I had to put up and shut up or risk a poor report on completion of my stint with the safety team.

After stopping for lunch and a delay following a couple of issues with the 30mm cannons on the Warriors, we were underway with the second platoon attack – the platoon attack that would see me bleeding out from an arterial wound in the next few minutes.

The range started similarly to that of the previous platoon. However, on this occasion, the section I'd followed through the trench system became the assaulting section, advancing onto the first compound. Just covering the open ground across to the compounds felt a bit of a cluster, and I found myself straining to hear a vague noise on the lad's radio next to me, added to the whistling and ringing of the ears that inevitably occurs on live firing ranges. The lads stacked up into their assaulting pairs that would clear the rooms in the compound to the left of the point of entry. From this point on, what was going on inside was only being communicated over the radios, so I was keen for this range to conclude, although maybe not in the way it did. I took my place behind the last assaulting pair and stood on the corner of the building. At this point, I was the furthest man forward and the least in the know.

On the first assaulting pair clearing the first room, several rounds came through the thin, temporary MDF wall and hit me. The pain I felt in that instant was one of intense burning and a cramp like never before in my right hamstring, which sent me crashing to the ground on my back. With fake casualties being called out during the ranges, my scream was greeted with confusion as to whether or not, "MAN DOWN" was being called for a genuine casualty or a role-play casualty. It soon became clear, though, when the safety staff member who went in with that first pair came out to find me spraying blood into the air from my leg. "STOP!" was called and what followed was ninety minutes of pain, humour, confusion, frustration and eventual relief.

Two lads, who I have such gratitude and admiration for, were quick to take control of the situation. Experienced soldiers Woody and

Spence (the latter being someone I will talk about in greater detail later in the book), who'd dealt with their fair share of genuine casualties on tours of Iraq and Afghanistan, were trying to reassure both myself and others, who were understandably in a state of shock. Unlike on operational tours, during training exercises the mind isn't prepared to see or deal with situations like this. On cutting my trousers off, a large exit wound the size of one of Andre the Giant's fists could be seen in my groin – not by myself, as they made sure I couldn't see the state of it. Spence had gone to apply pressure to the area with the palms of his hands, only for a hand to slip straight into the exit wound! So, he had to use his knees, which was horrendous. Tourniquets were applied above and below the exit wound, although I screamed more at that point than on the impact of being shot – my right testicle had been caught in one of the tourniquets, which strangely amused us all briefly.

They were spot on in everything they carried out, and are the reason I'm still here to have the opportunity to put this into words. The injuries were played down, and I was envied that I'd be in the pub later that evening. I was becoming restless, though – no one was carrying morphine pens on them, which meant I got to enjoy the full hardcore experience of laying with multiple gunshot wounds, tourniquets and a leg being kept elevated to stem the bleeding. This was frustrating me more than anything, as the pins and needles was agony, but I knew they were doing what was required. I could feel a hot, uncomfortable sensation in my right shoulder that I mentioned a couple of times before they decided to cut open my shirt. I'd been shot in my shoulder too, although it seemed quite a clean entry and exit, and it was packed with haemorrhage control.

I was now laying pretty much stark bollock naked on a stretcher, waiting for a helicopter to arrive to airlift me to hospital. I spoke a lot to Spence about not long being a dad, and I felt a strange, almost resigned, moment of warm, relaxed comfort in an otherwise hectic situation – a feeling I knew wasn't a good one, and which had obviously become apparent in my appearance. What followed was a jab to the face from Spence to bring me back around, and it did the trick. He would later tell me that my extremities had become blue, I was pale, my eyes had rolled back, and my jaw became relaxed – all bad signs. But, in those moments, I'd never felt such peace.

Eventually, the helicopter arrived – a Lynx, not the Chinook or Black Hawk you might expect to be picked up by in Iraq or Afghanistan, and there was a moment of further agony as the lads tried to squeeze me and the stretcher onto the Lynx.

Once on my way, initially to Medicine Hat Hospital, I felt safe and confident I'd now be okay – which was probably a mistake, as I then needed to be resuscitated on the helicopter. I flatlined for a full five minutes, needing the use of defibrillators to bring me back, and this had a knock-on effect far less visible than my leg. I suffered hypoxic injury: a lack of oxygen to the brain, which impacted my short-term memory. On landing, I remember nurses and doctors rushing over with a stretcher. I don't recall what followed, as I wouldn't come around until the 5th July 2011 – two days later.

Back home, Natalie received that knock at the door that she'd come to expect from the previous tours, but wasn't prepared for with me only on exercise in Canada. That knock came around 06:30 in the morning and our home at the time had a frosted glass panel on the front door. From the top of the stairs, she could see two men dressed in combats, and immediately prepared herself for the news that I'd been killed. The two soldiers had been sent from the nearest barracks, in Bicester, so they weren't Grenadiers and only had minimal information to pass on. She was then contacted by the Grenadier welfare team, and within hours she had to process what had happened, sort out childcare for Ellis, contact my dad and get to Heathrow Airport, where she and my dad were met and escorted straight onto a flight by a couple of lads from the welfare team. She said it was all happening in a blur and, up to that point, she still hadn't been told what sort of condition I was in.

As it turned out, that was because they didn't think I'd be alive by the time Natalie and my dad arrived in Canada.

I'd been flown to a hospital in Calgary that was better equipped to treat my injuries. I was completely unaware of that, and I'd wake up thinking I was still in Medicine Hat. Natalie and my dad arrived in Calgary and were met by the Padre from the regiment. It became apparent to them that their flight over was to involve the possibility of turning off my life support machine, as I'd gone into cardiac arrest on several occasions and required the use of defibrillators to bring me back. The loss of circulation, and my leg being all but dead from the time the tourniquets were put on, meant I was beginning to suffer with organ failure, and the drains attached to my leg were draining black fluid where gangrene had begun to set in.

Natalie has since explained to me that, being told I'd been shot in the arm and leg, she hadn't quite prepared herself for what she'd walk into. She burst into tears the first time she saw me as I lay there being kept alive solely by machines. I can't begin to imagine the thoughts that went through her head in those two days before I woke. On 5th July 2011, the decision was to try once again to wake me with the news that my time in the Grenadiers was over, something that would affect the rest of my life.

On opening my eyes, I saw Natalie and Dad stood there. Confused, I asked why they were in Medicine Hat and wanted to know where Ellis was. Ever the attentive husband, I noticed Natalie had her hair done, but as soon as I began to talk, a consultant stepped in with the bad news.

'We either amputate your leg today, Mark, or you won't see the day out.'

My heart sank and, initially, I refused permission – I knew losing my leg would be the end of my career. I'd never play football again, and it would impact all the things I'd looked forward to doing with my son.

The shock meant that I didn't shed a tear for a few weeks. On the one hand, I was so grateful that I was alive, but on the other, I hoped I could bluff the doctors into thinking my leg was okay. Some words of reality from Natalie and my dad hit home, and the thought that I wouldn't see Ellis again if I didn't have the amputation was enough to convince me it was the only option. Although that didn't stop me trying to bargain with the surgeon to only take it from below the knee.

And so, a green form of consent was put in front of me to sign and I was on my way to the theatre. I'd be taken back there more than once in the following days, as more and more leg was taken until they managed to get above the infection and salvage what was still alive. Before going into theatre, I said I could feel them squeezing my toes – I couldn't, but it was worth a shot!

Eventually, my leg was taken halfway up my thigh and my body began to respond. The colour came back into my face and I was showing signs of improving. The pain was unreal though, not from my leg so much, but from my gentleman's region. It had swollen to something worth bragging about had it not been so excruciating. Had they managed to curb the pain it was causing, the girth was a sight to be proud of! The added pain that the catheter was causing meant it was anything but pleasant, and it was a concern for the doctors, due to the sizeable hole left in my groin from the exit of the bullets. Still having no use of my right arm at this point, the nurses were required to turn me in my bed every few hours, which brought me to screaming in tears every single time. The male nurses were far more understanding and would move me in a way that didn't squash my manhood. One particular female nurse had zero empathy and would flip me like an omelette, which was made all the more degrading by the knowledge that on one occasion, my Company Sergeant Major was stood the other side of the curtain, having come to visit, and could hear what sounded like torturing taking place.

The days purely consisted of pain, and it reared its head in more ways than one. I had a breathing tube down my throat, which I tried to rip out, and as a result I had to be sedated and restrained. I was convinced that my right leg, which was clearly no longer there, was resting on a helmet, and I'd get aggravated with Natalie for leaving it sat under there. This was my first real experience of phantom limb pain, and the helplessness that came with not being able to take that pain away upset Natalie and often left me angry. Then came the catheter, something I never want to see attached to that part of me again! It would get caught on the side of the bed frame when I needed turning, causing a ripping, intense pain in an area that did not appreciate it one bit.

Natalie and my dad stayed with me for a few days after my amputation, before having to fly back to the UK. I'd slip in and out of sleep more often than not and would repeatedly ask if Natalie could sneak in something to drink. I was restricted to little sponge washes of my lips and I'd try to suck the fluids just to quench my thirst. I spent twelve days in Calgary before being flown to the Queen Elizabeth Hospital in Birmingham, where I was in the company of some of the most inspiring men I could have wished to meet. I was also surrounded by some of the finest doctors, nurses and surgeons our country had to offer.

22nd January 2011: The day Ellis Mark Smith, my son, was born

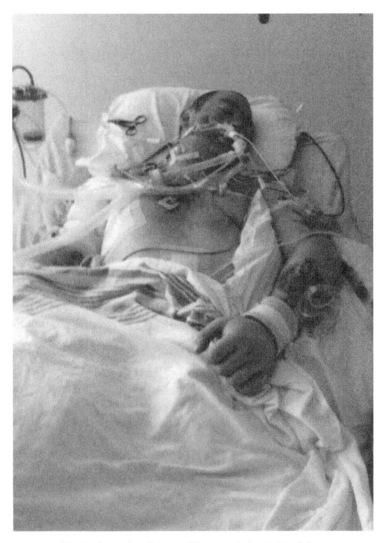

The day I was shot. Lying on life support in hospital in Calgary

10

WARD 412

The flight back to the UK was a painful one, crammed onto a small jet with two medics, and I was "nil by mouth" for the entire flight, due to the likelihood that I'd need surgery on arrival at Birmingham. I was then blue-lighted in the back of an ambulance, and I didn't feel in a good way at all – every speed bump felt like another gunshot wound. I felt hot, clammy, dehydrated and in almost as much pain as when I was shot. On arrival at the hospital, I was back in theatre and close to losing my penis. Had that been the outcome, I think "do not resuscitate" would have been the best option. The skin had begun to split from the continued swelling over the past two weeks, and there was a very real possibility of amputation. Even if that could be avoided, it was explained to me that there was a chance I wouldn't be able to have any more children. The leg needed yet more taking from it, including most of the remaining muscle tissue. The good news was, my shoulder had begun to improve and I had the use of my hand again.

I then spent another stint in intensive care under the influence of various drugs, the hallucinations from which led me to believe I was laying under a carousel of pink elephants, along with other strange scenarios. Natalie visited me in intensive care, but Ellis wasn't allowed down, and this gave me my first bit of real drive to get to a state well enough to be up on ward 412. In the early stages of my time in intensive care, Natalie was told I might not have any use of the leg stump, as I hadn't moved it at all. I remember her bursting into tears in front of me and me not really understanding why until it was explained. Then I made the effort to tense the leg ever so slightly, and a small spasm moved it. It was less than a baby step, but it gave me a determination to continue practicing tensing the leg in bed.

This progressed onto lifting it no more than an inch high, which felt agonising in the back of my thigh. A visit from the physiotherapists had me attempting to sit up and try to stand next to the bed – I must have lasted all of thirty seconds! I felt dizzy and lightheaded, and the throbbing pain from my leg hanging and not laying on a bed felt excruciating, and I was quickly exhausted. It was a mixture of emotions – Natalie was crying with optimism that I'd walk again, I was happy I could stand, but I was also disheartened that a task as simple as standing would exhaust me to the point of needing a bottle of brandy.

Another thing Natalie had been told was that my fitness levels at the time of my injury helped my body to cope with the trauma, and these words echoed in my head for some time. Keeping fit had played a part in helping me stay alive; it was nowhere near as important as the blokes who'd helped me, but it felt from that moment that I owed something to fitness. A visit from the Regimental Sergeant Major in intensive care left more of a bitter taste than the morphine, as his priority was for the three-week beard that had grown on my face to be removed by the time he came again. I laughed it off, only to have a nurse then come along with a cardboard bowl and the bluntest Bic razor she could find and shave me. It left me considering what was truly important to the army, as some hours previous the lad opposite me had passed away.

Not all Grenadiers were on the Sgt Major's level – our welfare officer, Captain Iain Farrell, went above and beyond his role, looking after Ellis to allow Natalie to come down and visit me. Spending hour upon hour at the hospital caring about me said a lot about him as a man and not just a welfare officer. For that, he will always hold a special place in mine and my family's hearts. I can't thank him enough for being there at a time when I needed some reassurance from the regiment that I wasn't another number to be thrown onto the scrapheap as surplus to requirements – something that men in the hospital from other regiments said they were envious of. The day that I was considered well enough to head from intensive care and up onto ward 412, he seemed just as excited as me, as he knew just how much I'd wanted to see Ellis, and he asked if he could do the honours of wheeling my bed up onto the ward.

I was taken into a room with some of the most inspiring men I've ever met. Opposite me was a corporal from the Royal Marines called Matt, more commonly known as Spider. He was a triple amputee, missing both legs and an arm above the elbow. Yet he was up and about in his wheelchair like he was nursing a broken toe. His positivity was infectious and, from the moment we got talking, my mindset became more positive – after all, I had three of my four limbs still intact. He motivated me more than I could ever thank him for. In the corner of the room was Bruce, an officer from the RLC whose vehicle had hit an IED while he was on top cover, and he was unsure if he'd keep his leg. Again, he couldn't have been more upbeat and down to earth. I have no doubt that coming into that room played a huge part in where this journey has taken me.

No sooner had we got talking than Natalie and my dad came in and there was Ellis – now six months old. I thought I'd be unrecognisable to him, but there he was, with the biggest of smiles for me. I sat up in bed and Natalie put him on my lap, and I showered him with kisses. But he had other ideas – curiosity got the better of him when he spotted the canular in my hand and he ripped it out. Cue blood and Natalie quickly taking him back!

Those first few weeks up on the ward were great – taking baby steps of progress, firstly into a wheelchair, then getting around the hospital, although I had to bring my man bag of drains and vacuum packs that were still attached to my leg with me. I loved being mobile enough to race down to the hospital restaurant in my wheelchair, where the food was much nicer, and being able to feed Ellis in his highchair.

I had lads from the Grenadiers coming to visit daily. I'm sure they used to time their visits to coincide with the arrival of the cake lady, who those blokes will remember with a lot of fondness. She gave up her time once a week to bring in a trolley of home-made cakes, although that metallic morphine taste meant I rarely enjoyed them to their full potential. Tuesday evenings were Domino's night as well, so I'd always have a full group of visitors in my bed space, and the bloke bringing the trolley round would offer left-over pizza to the people visiting. He was mega, a Royal Anglian who'd lost his leg in Iraq – a real inspiration who showed us just how well we might walk one day on a prosthetic.

Trips to the operating theatre were still a regular occurrence, but I almost began to enjoy going down – not for the operation or the discomfort that would follow, but I actually began to like the feeling of the anaesthetic being injected up my arm and the gas I'd get to breath in beforehand. I was on first name terms with the staff in there and found the feeling of tranquillity as I dozed off quite relaxing. The less relaxing moments came when I had fifty staples removed from my leg, which formed a scar from my hip, down the leg and around, and up into my groin. I was thankful that I had little feeling in the areas from where the staples were being removed.

The phantom pain I'd experienced in Canada was one that hadn't died down. If anything, it had intensified and would keep me awake most nights. Getting comfortable would only really happen about ten minutes before the morning nurses came around at 06:00 to take blood and dish out the medication. I got found out for throwing the meds behind my bed rather than taking them, as they made food taste like metal. If I did fall asleep during the day,

I'd be woken up – "Mark, we need to take some bloods."

I began to hate those words, as my body resembled that of a drug addict. It reached the point of needing a surgeon from the burns ward to come and do my bloods, as so many of my veins had collapsed.

I'd been positive from the moment I got up onto the ward, but Natalie knew it was inevitable that wouldn't last. I'd almost taken comfort in the fact that the leg was giving me pain, as it meant what was left was still alive. I had an overwhelming desire to bend my knee, the same knee that was five thousand miles away in a furnace in Canada. Mirror therapy was suggested, to trick the brain into thinking I had two legs – placing a tall mirror next to my left leg (the good one) and bending that. It seemed worth a try, even if I was slightly sceptical, but it worked. I felt relaxed for the first time since the amputation. The urges to bend my right leg had been testing my temper up to then, but now my mind, if nothing else, felt lighter, and I managed to sleep.

The morning that followed brought with it my first real low point, and I didn't really see it coming. My bedside table was placed across me with my breakfast, and it was as if it was day one. I looked down and felt no pain, as the effects of the mirror therapy had helped. Beneath the bedside table, I could see only one leg sticking out and, for the first time, I cried – properly cried. It hit me harder than those bullets did, looking down and finally processing that my leg was gone. Up to that point, I'd focussed on the positives. I was alive, I was making progress, I was surrounded by visitors daily and I hadn't really taken time to accept what the long-term implications of this would be. It all hit me at once – I'd been kidding myself and others that I could still have a role in Battalion.

When Natalie came in with Ellis for her visit, I poured my heart out to her that I didn't know what I was going to do with my life once this was all done. I'd been so distracted by the optimism of making progress that I hadn't really thought of the finer details – like an income beyond the army and the security of a roof over our heads. Suddenly all the negatives rushed to the surface and it got the better of me. I still hadn't really looked at my leg, I just kept it hidden. I couldn't look at the hole in my groin and I couldn't look at the catheter in my penis.

I was losing weight – the metallic taste from the morphine meant that even when I wasn't "nil by mouth", I had zero appetite. I still couldn't get up on crutches, as the gunshot to my shoulder meant I didn't have the strength to hold myself up, and this was a real test of my dignity. The morphine, as well as killing off my taste buds, also constipated me, and it meant I'd gone weeks without a shit. To say I was uncomfortable was an understatement and so I needed an enema, which the others found pretty amusing, hearing the noises that came through the less-than-soundproof curtain around my bed.

I was given a cardboard bowl and was expected to hold myself up to empty my bowels into it, but the staples in my shoulder split, and I dropped and sat in my own shit in the bowl. I needed to be taken to the showers and washed down by the nurses, where my last little bit of dignity was flushed away. That was as low as it could get, or so I thought – until my catheter, which had now been in some six weeks or so, became blocked. I was wriggling and fidgeting in bed like I was possessed. The need to go for a piss wouldn't subside and I was sweating more than I had in the heat of Iraq. Natalie turned up for visiting time to see me in a state that was similar to when I was in intensive care. The decision was taken to remove my catheter, which I'm positive grew needles and claws. It felt like it was ripping my soul out when it was removed and I filled four piss bottles to the top before falling asleep, relieved.

Having relied on the catheter to do the work of the bladder for me, I inevitably pissed the bed for the next few days and nights. I really felt bad for the nurses who had to keep changing my bedding. On the third time of pissing the bed in one night, I decided to lie in it until morning to avoid having to press my buzzer again. I've known blokes in Battalion to piss the bed after a heavy night's drinking, so that wasn't the issue – it was relying on someone else to clean it all up for me that felt degrading. This experience meant that, on the operation to finally close up the exit wound in my groin, I asked not to be fitted with a catheter. I weighed up the feeling of pissing in bottles in bed compared to having to go through having a catheter removed again – there was no contest!

Spending the summer months in a room with big windows that barely opened and the sun beating through made me desperate to get outside and enjoy some fresh air. I'd been in this hospital for weeks and had no idea what the outside even looked like. With all my drains detangled and hanging from my wheelchair, I made my way down the corridor to the lifts. I couldn't wait to breathe in fresh air, once past the smoking area, but my spirits fell when a lady opted to wait for another lift. She seemed mortified by the fact that my leg (what was left of it) was on show. I had the drains coming from it so I couldn't wear trousers, only shorts. She made it quite clear that she didn't want to see the state of my leg. This created an awkward atmosphere in the lift for those who were left in with me. I suppose they were embarrassed for me, but they didn't say anything – and neither did I.

Now that I'd experienced the euphoria of fresh air, I wanted to spend as much time as possible outside. A few of us were offered the opportunity to head out of the hospital grounds and go to Norton House to spend lunchtime with our wives. Norton House was close to the Queen Elizabeth Hospital and was funded by SSAFA, the Forces charity, to offer a residence to the next of kin of injured soldiers. Natalie was really excited to show me where she and Ellis had been living, and Spider's wife made a Thai curry for the few of us who were coming in a minibus. I wasn't feeling particularly great that day, which led to me face planting on the floor when trying to transfer from my bed to my wheelchair, in front of the physios. They were reluctant to let me leave the ward after that, and insisted on escorting me.

Our weekly weigh-ins had seen me lose weight week on week, to the point where I became unrecognisable to lads I'd served alongside. I dropped to my lowest, 61kg, half of what I would go on to weigh in Strongman. The sight of my wasted body in the mirror affected me more than losing my leg and undoubtedly influenced my decision to eventually step onto a bodybuilding stage. I vowed to myself that once I was finally well enough to get to Headley Court, the military rehabilitation centre where I'd get walking, I'd never look that ill again.

The daily ward rounds were where every doctor and his dog would surround us in bed and talk about us between themselves, almost like we weren't there. I'd often have to ask a nurse to translate what they said into normal speak. A concern of theirs during ward rounds was that, during my physio sessions, my lack of adductor muscles meant my leg uncontrollably fell to the right whenever lifted into the air, and it was supposed that this would make it difficult to control a prosthetic leg. It brought my stubbornness to the surface and obsessed me for the next two days, and I spent every spare minute in bed trying to control the remaining muscles in my leg to stop the stump from falling to the right.

In total, I spent twelve weeks in hospital, between Calgary and the Queen Elizabeth Hospital, watching others make the next step on to Headley Court. I began to pester them daily to get to that place, and I was going to put in all the effort needed to get walking.

Then it happened!

I was ecstatic to be discharged from hospital and to have a few days at home before starting at Headley Court. Our home was far from adapted and getting around in a wheelchair was a non-starter. The hospital gave me a stool for the bathroom, to allow me to sit and wash, and a bath bench meant I could relax in the bath. But I wasn't strong enough to get up our stairs on crutches and that first night had me bum shuffling up the steps backwards, with Natalie following to make sure I was safe. I burst into tears at the top – here I was, the man of our house, meant to protect my family and often called her "big, brave soldier" by Natalie, and I couldn't even tackle a set of stairs.

It was a low point, but it spurred me on to work hard.

August 2011: My first time outside of the hospital ward, and the photograph that kickstarted my determination to push myself

11

OUR LITTLE MIRACLE

On my first day at Headley Court, lads who'd been there a while all looked so much healthier than when I'd seen them in hospital. Some of these people I hadn't known prior to being in with them, so didn't really know how they'd looked before their injuries. I'd seen them at their worst and this place was certainly helping them get back to something like their best. I'd also only known some lads in wheelchairs and had become used to seeing them at a certain height, so to see them up and about on prosthetic legs and taller than me was strange. I felt so positive from the offset – it was clearly visible here that I would make progress if I put the effort in.

Being shown around to familiarise myself, it instantly felt more of a military set up. Physical training instructors, lessons, structured timetables and morning and afternoon roll calls. It was exactly where I wanted and needed to be at that time. Headley Court was set in amazing grounds, beautiful gardens and historical buildings, with the best facilities the military could buy. There were purpose-built swimming pools, physiotherapy departments, mental health practitioners, occupational therapists, social workers and some of the best prosthetists the country had to offer. We couldn't be found wanting for anything, in truth.

On the completion of my tour, the nurse who'd shown me around asked if I had any questions, and I didn't hesitate to ask if I was allowed to make my way to the gym. At that point I was weak, feeble and barely nine stone in bodyweight. With the gunshot wound to my shoulder, I wasn't strong enough to support myself on crutches, so I was still in a wheelchair and I had a vacuum pack attached to my leg, as the end of the stump was still an open wound and the femur could be partially seen, which would delay me getting up onto a prosthetic for a while.

I made my way down to the gym, as the rest of the day was mainly paperwork before starting to meet the people who would play a big role in not only helping me to walk and run again, but in giving me the best opportunity possible to be successful beyond my time in the military. It felt knackering to use any of the gym equipment, and the gunshot wound in my shoulder was giving me some grief. I couldn't have been further from someone who would one day be pulling trucks, and I'm pretty sure that if I'd suggested that on that first day, they'd have put it down to the medication.

I was on a lot of meds, which was one of the first things I wanted to change. The checklist included tramadol, pregabalin, amitriptyline, diclofenac and oromorph, and ridiculously high amounts of the stuff. One thing the military doctors weren't tight on was dosages, but I wanted to come off them as soon as possible. I wanted to get driving again, not to rely on my wife or people from the Grenadiers to drive me everywhere or pick me up on a Friday afternoon – I can't imagine many blokes were thrilled at being given that job. While on all the meds, I barely felt alert enough to steer my wheelchair, never mind a car.

That first night was a rough one, I hadn't been told we had to sort our own medication out. In hospital, it was just brought to us as and when we were told to take it. I was climbing the walls, as I essentially went cold turkey for the night and lay in a cold sweat, wriggling around like a in scene from trainspotting or the exorcist.

I followed the crowds to breakfast and roll call, as I'd already forgotten where anywhere was. Something that has been less than visible, but at times caused more issues than my leg, is my memory loss. My short-term memory, as a result of the hypoxic injury, was horrendous – names and directions from two minutes ago were already somewhere in the abyss. They might reappear in a couple of minutes or never be seen again. It was more frustrating than my prosthetic leg at times, even if it did come with the perk of not carrying out chores I was asked to do at home.

And so, as everyone disappeared off in the direction of their first session, I had no idea where to go. The day started at 08:00 and finished at 16:30, with a couple of breaks in between. While others saw those breaks as a chance to sleep, watch television and eat, I started sneaking off to the gym, and this became almost addictive. I was beginning to find the gym a therapeutic place, somewhere to start the baby steps that would help me mentally and physically – I was hellbent on not looking as ill as I had in hospital.

I enjoyed the routine that came with our individual timetables and, as with each admission at Headley Court, we were asked for our goals, both long and short term. Each admission tended to be a three-to-six-week residential stay, going home at weekends, with a break before the next admission. My goals didn't really vary from one to the next – get walking, then get walking with no stick, get running on a blade, plenty of swimming. I tried to get into the swimming session every afternoon, along with plenty of gym time.

Walking began with what felt like a bit of an anti-climax, although a visit from Natalie really pushed me on to show off how far I'd come. She'd seen me in Canada, in Birmingham and had seen me struggle at home, so it was nice to have her see the continuing progress. This came through an inflatable leg, known as a PAM Aid (post amputation mobility aid); as high tech as it sounds. The leg attached to my stump with a solid, fixed frame and a stick that was inflated until it couldn't fall off. There was no knee bend and no ditching the crutches, but I felt ten-foot-tall when walking between the bars on my inflatable leg for Natalie to see. And there was Ellis, sat in his buggy, smiling away and enjoying the attention that came with it.

Although I had short-term goals that I believed to be achievable, I was no closer to having any idea what my long-term future would be. I'd come to accept that it wouldn't be in the military, but I did want to continue to do something physically demanding. That mindset hadn't changed from my teenage self who dreamt of an active career.

I knew Headley Court was a place where you get out what you put in and, although I applied this physically and when it came to getting up and about on crutches, I had the opposite mindset when it came to mental health. I was in a place where 99% of the patients were injured in Afghanistan and where the majority of them were double amputees, as well as some who'd lost their genitals, their sight, an arm, the ability to walk at all – and here I was, only missing a leg. So I felt like I had no right to complain, no right to say I was struggling, even more so because of how I was injured. It was something I was almost embarrassed about. Natalie was keen for me to take up the offer of counsellor sessions while at Headley, but she was met with defiance. I took it as a suggestion that I was weak, soft, and so I attended the appointments that we had to attend and ticked the boxes that would mean I didn't need to waste anyone's time. I didn't feel like I had any right to moan about the cards Id been dealt when I was surrounded by people who were genuine heroes in my eyes.

There was also an underlying sense that a single leg amputation was only a flesh wound, a scratch, bluffing it. It created a mentality that would only cause me more pain in the future, pain that would have been avoidable if I'd listened to my wife more rather than allowing that Headley mentality to cloud my common sense. There was a mindset, that if you had a prosthetic leg, you should be on it and it should be on you – being in a wheelchair was lazy – crutches were an easy option. This was something my pride wouldn't let me break away from, no matter how much pain I was in or how much it impacted those close to me, often negatively.

I avoided the trips the military charities put on, as I just wanted to focus on the gym, getting walking and driving. In my first admission at Headley, I said I felt like a burden on others who had to drive me everywhere, so I wanted to sit my driving assessment to see what adaptations I would need and to get the ball rolling with buying an adapted car. The assessment was less like a test and more a chance to try out hand controls. For me, missing a right leg, an automatic car with an accelerator on the left seemed fine, until it came to left foot braking. Cue drivers following me, shitting themselves as I performed more than one emergency stop.

My first admission came to an end, and it certainly felt like a positive one. Walking on a PAM aid leg, swimming, using the gym and driving. But I was to be away from Headley for a while, as I needed two operations: 1) to take some more off my leg, so that it could finally be closed up and heal enough to be fitted with a proper prosthetic, and 2) far more traumatic, I'd be getting circumcised! Believe me, that terrified me a lot more than losing more of my leg – I kind of welcomed that, as it had been holding me back from walking.

The circumcision was necessary, but the thought of a surgeon using a scalpel in that region was enough to leave me requiring two lots of general anaesthetic on the day of that particular surgery – something the anaesthetists couldn't quite understand, given I was missing a leg and had been shot in the shoulder. What made it worse was the circumcision was done on our wedding anniversary. That region, a bloke would hope, gets some special treatment on a wedding anniversary, and this was certainly not what I had in mind. But it was needed, as there was almost as much foreskin as actual penis. The swelling I'd suffered so painfully in Canada had had an adverse effect on the appearance of my dick, but that didn't make the thought of the circumcision any easier. I woke up to find it resembled Mr Bump from the Mr Men books, with its own little bloodied blue bandage.

Just when I thought my dignity couldn't be dented any more.

I was told I should avoid erections for around four weeks, to allow the stitches to do their job. I failed that on the very first morning and I knew all about it!

The time at home, waiting for both my leg and penis to heal, gave me an opportunity to wean myself off all the meds I was on. When it came to me going back to Headley for my next admission, I was able to drive there, having bought an adapted car. It gave me so much independence back and I wanted to feel alert on the road. It was a painful, tiring five days to adjust to no medication and, with the amount I was on, I probably didn't go about it in the most sensible way. I'm quite a stubborn person, and in some ways that has served me well, but in the nights that followed, it would have been easier to head downstairs and take some tramadol, just to get some sleep.

The pain I initially felt was something that had evidently been masked by the medication, but I found I could wake up and not have to feel like death for the next two hours while I waited for the amitriptyline to wear off. The pros outweighed the cons. I could start the day a lot more positive and energetic and, despite numerous operations and pain since then, late 2011 was the last time I took any medication for my leg.

I was recovering and wanting to see how my new-look penis would work, especially given that we'd been told there was a possibility I wouldn't be able to father any more children. We'd spoken for some time about trying for another baby and, to our surprise, the penis was more effective than ever. Natalie was soon pregnant and expecting our second child. I guess she'd probably have worded that far better than I just did, but we were both in tears of joy as she took the test. I had to get walking now, as I wanted to carry this little one out of hospital in the same way I had with Ellis – car seat in hand and proud as could be.

I was back in Headley Court for January 2012 and, with a fully-healed leg, I could really get stuck into this walking lark. One thing that sucked day after day while on an admission was definitely physio. With nerve endings damaged and most muscles taken or wasting away, I had patches of my leg that were completely numb. Other parts were hypersensitive, and I wasn't keen on letting anyone touch them. I'd lost my hamstring, so the sensation of the back of my leg stump being touched, scratched or massaged was one that made me feel sick. I tried acupuncture, which I'd been told might make me fall asleep as it would be so relaxing – it definitely wasn't!

My biggest discomfort when it came to finding a suitable prosthesis came from the exit wound in my groin. It felt like the carbon fibre was pinging an elastic band with each step. I had next to no tissue or fat between the bone and the skin, which was covered in scar tissue. I can only liken a socket for a prosthetic leg to a pair of stilettos – you can walk on them, get used to them, but you can't wait to take them off in the evening.

Once I started walking, it became clear to the consultants and prosthetists that the lack of remaining muscle meant I'd struggle on a leg that didn't offer much in the way of stability. My first prosthetic was a KX06, quite a high activity leg, but pretty unstable if you lacked strong glutes and adductor muscles. My glute was shot several times and my adductors were gone completely, so I never progressed beyond a walking stick and would fall if I wasn't 100% concentrating, which was mentally exhausting.

My perseverance and effort didn't go unnoticed. As someone who was keen to be as active as possible, it gave me the opportunity to trial plenty of legs. Prosthetic limb companies would come in wanting the contract to provide wounded soldiers with legs, so the technology seemed to develop rapidly. I'd take legs home and put them through their paces and give my feedback, as would several other lads. Some I enjoyed walking on, some took forever to set up and I just couldn't get on with. But, towards the end of my stint at Headley, a great leg was introduced and I loved it. It provided me with the perfect stability to carry my son's car seat, carry the shopping, walk without a stick, lift weights in the gym and have more all-round input at home.

In total, I spent two years at Headley Court, but it became a much tougher place for me to be when the Grenadier Guards deployed on Herrick 16 to Afghanistan in 2012. I'd been one of the only Grenadiers at Headley at the time, given the circumstances of how my injury came about, and I was predominantly there with Royal Marines. But the 2012 tour was particularly hard on the Grenadiers, and these lads began to filter through into rehabilitation. I used my time there to try to set an example for them, to show the progress they could make and just generally try to keep their spirits high as they came to terms with their injuries. It gave me an incentive to raise my own standards in the hope of that rubbing off on them, just as those lads I shared a room with in hospital had unknowingly done for me.

We'd head out every week, all the Grenadiers, for food and beers, and I'd offer to drive and carry their wheelchairs and whatever else was needed to help. The regiment lost a further five men on Herrick 16, and what seemed like countless numbers made their way to Headley Court with life changing injuries. But they did themselves and the regiment proud in how they tackled it all head on. I was proud to be able to say that I served in the same regiment as fine men like that.

Back home, our handsome little miracle, Ethan James Smith, was born on 4th August 2012, and he certainly put my own setbacks into context. Natalie woke to heavy bleeding, despite not being due to give birth for another three weeks. We rushed to the hospital, where we were told that she was haemorrhaging and the labour would need to be induced. This was more harrowing to me than any of the problems I'd had. Seeing Natalie in distress and worrying if Ethan would be okay was all that mattered. But he came into the world fit and healthy and reduced me to an emotional mess, after worrying that I'd lose them both.

As with Ellis, I took Ethan, held him up by the window, welcomed him to the world and sat beaming with pride giving him his first bottle of milk. Unlike with Ellis's birth, though, I didn't have to rush off. My consultant was brilliant and gave me the chance to enjoy all the little moments I felt I'd missed out on before. Having used my previous admission to practice carrying a car seat, I was even walking well enough to carry Ethan in his car seat down the stairs and to the car. It meant a lot that my physios made time in my rehabilitation to allow me to practice for that moment. But the complications that came with his birth and the pain Natalie had been in meant our family was now complete.

We would have no more children.

I had more than just a spring in my step heading back for my next admission. I love being a dad and feel privileged to have two healthy, happy boys, and it felt great to know that I'd be around to be involved more this time. I couldn't stop looking at him the first night we got him home, knowing that if it wasn't for all the people who played their part in keeping me alive, this little man wouldn't exist.

On every admission, I'd been talking up my desire to run again, and I kept pestering them for a running blade. I eventually wore my consultant down – he'd been concerned that the lack of muscle and strength in my stump wouldn't make me an ideal person to progress to running, but I kept asking every week for almost two years. To tell the truth, I just wanted to experience it once, to scratch that itch, to get it out of my system, to feel out of breath and have that cold lung feeling that definitely didn't come with the pace I walked at on a normal prosthetic leg.

I'm proud to say that my last full day at Headley Court consisted of me completing 400 metres of a running track on a blade. It was nowhere near worthy of anything you'd see at the Paralympics or the Invictus Games but, to me, I could tick that box and be proud I'd done it. It was agony really, due to the spring in the blade – the leg needed to be a few inches higher, so my hips and back were in bits. Being an above knee amputee meant I had what was known as a "free knee", so it provided no support at all and needed to be fully flicked forward and locked out before it landed to avoid face planting the track – which was a common occurrence.

Elsewhere in my rehabilitation, I was also learning coping techniques for my abysmal short-term memory. I could shake someone's hand and learn their name, only to forget it before we even finished speaking. This was made all the more embarrassing if I was then asked to introduce the person to my wife, for example, as I wouldn't have a clue what their name was. I still use a lot of the technique every day now, repeating people's names back to them in conversation, keeping to-do lists, setting alarms so as to not miss appointments, leaving post-it notes in places. I've been told by more than one person, but mainly my wife, that I've regularly related the same story five or six times. At first she thought I was taking the piss, until she realised I had no idea I'd told her the exact same story less than an hour previous. I have no idea how many times I've done this or who has just been polite and listened more than once – so apologies for any repetition in this book!

Having progressed with my walking and having had the chance to run, as well as finding ways to come to terms with my short-term memory, I was in a much better state than when I arrived at Headley Court. I'd pretty much got what I felt I needed from my rehabilitation and began to feel like I was stuck at a crossroads. I was a soldier, but only by job title – I no longer served in Battalion and never would again. But I wasn't a civilian either, so I felt at a point that most blokes reach, where they need some direction. Most men had an idea of a career they wanted to pursue after their medical discharge, but I was lost, I still had no idea. I was beginning to be pressured slightly by the occupational therapists, who were keen to help get me onto the appropriate course that would re-train me for life after the military, but I could only answer with "something to do with sport".

I was adamant that, despite being an amputee, I didn't want to sit at a desk. I was proactive in my time at home between admissions, enrolling myself on coaching courses with the Army Football Association and the Amateur Boxing Association, as well as completing a six-week course to become a qualified personal trainer. Although, soon after officially leaving the army, I'd realise there was a vast difference between training in a gym and working in one.

My medical board was held in Aldershot, in front of four high ranking officers and medical professionals. A medical board is a meeting with military representatives, officers and medical professionals who assess injuries and the possibility of returning to work; they evaluate the likelihood of an individual being able to continue in a role in the army. If that's unlikely, then a medical discharge is offered. I took the decision to accept a medical discharge. This would ensure both myself and my family would be financially supported for the remainder of my life and that my pension would start as soon as I was discharged. Having that security was a big factor. But it was a day when I felt more than a lump in my throat, knowing that was it – officially, I'd no longer be a serving soldier. On my last day I handed in my army ID and, from that point on, I'd no longer be able to just stroll into the barracks – I'd be a civilian that would need escorting.

Being medically discharged was the logical pathway. I'd seen friends lose limbs and stay in, only to regret that decision, as their role drastically changed. That played a big part in my decision when it came to my own medical board. Medically downgraded lads who stayed in were relegated to "non-deployable". If I couldn't be an infantry soldier anymore, it would have more of a negative effect on me to stay in the regiment, take up an administrative role and see all the blokes going away on operational tours and out on PT and exercise, while being stuck in the barracks.

I'd served ten years in the army all over the world, guarded Buckingham Palace and made lifelong friends, so I was able to hold my head high, especially after how I persevered to pass selection in the first place as a young man. I loved almost every second and life will never be quite as much of an adrenaline rush as it was in places like Afghanistan, nor will I meet many people like the men I've been so proud to serve alongside. Knowing that I'll never be in that career again, I do feel that, although I survived my injuries, a part of me was left in Canada with my leg.

Before I sign off on this particular chapter, I'd like to thank all the people who got me to a point where I was well enough to be discharged and head out into the world as a veteran. The lads who kept me alive at the time of my injury, the men and women of Medicine Hat, Calgary and Queen Elizabeth Hospitals, their work and efforts were, and continue to be, amazing. The gratitude I have towards each of you and the part you've all played in allowing me the chance to be a husband and a dad will never be forgotten or overlooked – I literally owe you all my life.

To all the staff at Headley Court – I was probably one of the most irritating patients at times, as my sockets posed some challenges. Although, hands and fingers in awkward places in prosthetics when being plaster cast was probably my well-deserved comeuppance. Let me explain: in order to get the best-fitting socket for a leg, the ischium bone has to be located, to allow that bone to bear weight – as opposed to the end of the stump doing the job, which can be very painful. Locating the ischium bone means a finger or two in very close proximity to the anus – if you get my drift.

Scary stuff!

All joking aside, as British soldiers, I truly believe we have some of the best post-injury care in the world and I never wanted for anything in that respect. Everyone employed at Headley Court gave me the confidence to walk and accomplish physical challenges that wouldn't have been possible without each of your time and input.

Thank you!

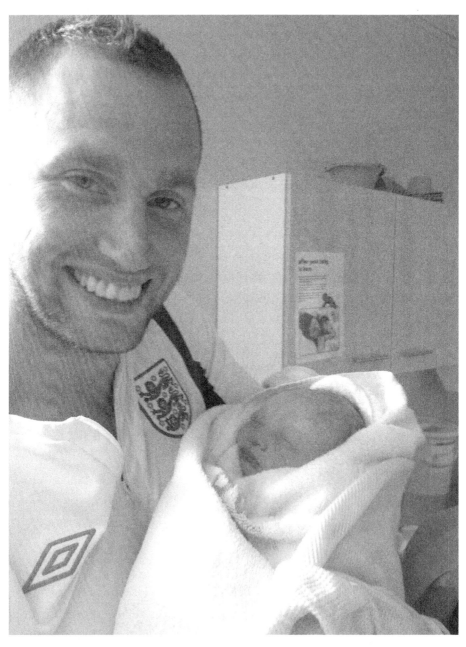

4th August 2012: The day Ethan James Smith, my son, was born

12

FINDING A PURPOSE

Having completed my personal trainer's qualification during my resettlement course, I was soon employed at Bannatynes Health Club which, as far as gyms went, seemed like a good place to learn and, hopefully, make a good name for myself. Within weeks, however, I was finding adjusting to civilian life a challenge. My wife and I were spending more time around each other than we normally would, and our differing habits and routines were taking some getting used to. In the past, leave had always been a whirlwind – knowing I'd soon be back at work, we used to plan plenty to do and places to visit. But this was normal life now, everyday husband and wife stuff, and I felt a little trapped as I came to terms with not having the barracks to return to as somewhere to have my own space. A lot of the friends I'd made in Battalion were either still serving or living in various parts of the country.

Don't get me wrong, I loved being more involved with my boys and I loved that I could sleep in our own bed every night, without the fear of being woken up in the middle of the night to go on stag in the cold and wet. That feeling has never worn off! But I was already finding that I needed more of a purpose and a challenge, something to excite me and get me out of bed in the morning. I didn't want my boys to grow up seeing a shadow of a man, but a role model that they could take some inspiration from. Someone to lead by example, in the same way that I'd wanted to as a Lance Sergeant.

Bannatynes was a nice gym, a bit more upmarket than the gym I was training at myself – I have a real soft spot for old spit-and-sawdust gyms, places with men I can learn from, look up to and really push myself. I had exactly that at Atlas Gym in Milton Keynes, its very walls covered in the logo and underlined with a slogan befitting of its feel – "Home of the Spartans". A venue that might have been considered intimidating to those unfamiliar with the amount of experienced, and knowledgeable and genuinely nice people that packed it out each day. Buckets on the floor caught rainwater when it fell, the deadlifting bars were cold to the touch on a winter's morning and it had that certain gym-bag smell to it – an aroma that bodybuilders, strongmen and powerlifters alike all seemed to be drawn to. I was no different. I wanted to be in the presence of men far stronger than me, I wanted to learn from them in the same way that I wanted to learn from leaders in the Battalion who I admired. The two gyms couldn't have been more contrasting. Bannatynes housed its own spa, pool, beauty salon and yoga classes, and its members were predominantly businessmen in suits, who often changed into the dressing gowns provided at the desk on arrival.

I was working 14:00-22:30 shifts, which was a little frustrating, as it meant I wouldn't see my boys much during the week. Despite it being quite a warm gym, with the humidity from the pool and sauna overpowering the floor, I was expected to wear long sleeve tops, as my tattoos were considered off-putting to the fee-paying members. I was beginning to struggle for motivation early on in this new career, and, with the gym manager keen for all personal trainers to be ever-present on the gym floor, I was struggling with my leg from my second week in. The constant standing was causing my stump to swell. This wasn't going to be a role I could see myself fulfilling for the next three months, never mind the next thirty years or so.

In terms of the role itself, I wanted to help people, to help them grow in confidence and boost their self-esteem. I believed that seeing someone who was missing a leg would have a positive effect. If I joined in with each and every session, people would see me cracking on and it would motivate them. My shifts tended to be busy, with two to three gym inductions, familiarising new members with how to use the equipment safely and offering to help with any nutritional or training advice people wanted. As I was paid by the gym, I opted to offer these at no extra cost, as it seemed extortionate that these members paid a lot to train here and the gym wanted even more money for personal training sessions on top – money that the personal trainers took only a small percentage of.

I was expected to assist in the regular checks and cleaning of the pool and jacuzzi and in taking some group classes. My first of these was a little disheartening to say the least – when I was introduced to the class as the instructor, the majority walked out almost immediately. I guess they weren't so encouraged by my lacking a right leg as I thought they would be. If my time wasn't taken with inductions or the odd group, it was spent tidying up after people who wouldn't re-rack their weights, which could be a real test of patience. One late evening, not long before the gym was due to close, a couple of lads left just about every dumbbell on the floor and told me it was my job to put them away. That comment was the one that made my mind up that this wasn't the path for me.

Disillusioned at what working in a gym was actually like, I realised that enjoying training in one and working in one were two very different experiences. I particularly didn't enjoy wiping pubic hairs and sweat off treadmills, and one moment that horrified most the staff, but which the squaddie in me found highly amusing, was finding a massive shit sat there in the middle of the men's showers. I still wonder who left it behind and why – couldn't they make it to the toilet, which was only a few feet away? As funny as this would have been in the barracks, it really made me question if this is what I could be doing for the foreseeable future. Thankfully, I was on a probationary period of three months and I'd been discussing other options with Natalie, as I didn't feel like this was my purpose in life.

I wanted more.

I'd been at one of the most inspirational places you could wish to be, in Headley Court, surrounded by men pushing themselves beyond their limitations and physically exerting themselves daily. People coming to terms with life changing injuries who just smiled and sweated out any self-pity. It was a much tougher ask to motivate people who perhaps didn't share my drive and enthusiasm. Words of encouragement and joining in with each exercise weren't enough, and to be honest, I lacked the empathy required at that point in my life to be the person those people needed. Looking back, I was still a soldier and I found myself expecting others to be as motivated as myself. It was strange to hear phrases like "I can't," and my efforts of encouragement weren't nearly enough to help them.

I began to really miss the army and resented this job, as each time I got in my car to head to the gym, it was time I could have been spending with my wife and boys. And so, I sat down with my oracle, Natalie, the lady who had the sensible, logical answers for all my troubles. I said I needed a challenge and that I'd been in awe of the vastly experienced bodybuilders at Atlas and found myself hanging off their every word, enjoying the years of experience that they had both in and out of the gym. That image of myself at 61kg in hospital, ill, malnourished and weak, still fuelled my diet, my training and my mind. And what better way to prove how far I'd come from that person than to put myself in the vulnerable position of being a bodybuilder, up on stage to be critiqued by judges and the crowd alike?

Milton Keynes doesn't have many amputees, so I had to get used to being stared early on. I needed to grow my self-confidence in my appearance, and I could think of no better way to do so than to stand on stage in very little and to be judged, not for what I was missing, but for all I still had. Even as these words left my mouth in conversation with Natalie, I could picture it. It excited me, following to some degree in the footsteps of a childhood hero of mine: Arnold Schwarzenegger.

We discussed if it was financially feasible for me to give up work, as I had my military pension and the gym job was mostly working to keep myself occupied and sane. I began looking at which competitions in England would allow an amputee to compete in. I found one called Pure Elite, to be held in Margate in November 2014. Not only would they welcome an amputee, it also had a disability class, which would allow me to be stood on stage alongside people overcoming their own various disabilities. This gave me a rocket up the backside, and I entered it online that very evening. I've always been someone who, if I say something out loud or publicly or enter something, I have to see it through. I enjoy putting that pressure on myself. If you're going to do it, do it! Don't just talk about doing it.

I had also, in a moment of enthusiasm, entered a 5km assault course, just as another challenge to embrace. I entered it on my crutches, without wearing my prosthetic leg and, regardless of where I'd finish, I was determined to complete every obstacle. I wanted to do it to raise money for BLESMA, the British Limbless Ex-Serviceman's Association. And so, I now had a bodybuilding show and a 5km assault course to fill the void that had become so prominent so soon after becoming a civilian. Natalie and some of my friends signed up too, and it was my first real step into proving what could be done on one leg.

I handed in my notice at Bannatynes and, to be fair, I looked far from capable of stepping onto a bodybuilding stage at that point, so I must have raised more than an few eyebrows when I discussed my ambitions. But that was part of the appeal – the challenge of proving people wrong, just as I had years ago when it came to joining the army. On my next training session at Atlas, I plucked up the courage to ask one of the bodybuilders, Tommo, renowned for competing in competitions like Mr Universe and widely respected in bodybuilding and in the gym, if he would help me prepare. I had just over six months to get ready, and I promised him that I'd live however he told me. If he'd said I could look a fraction of how good he looked on stage through sleeping an hour a night and staring directly into the sun, I'd have done it!

He'd helped others in the gym in their preparation and they all spoke so highly of him. From their photos, they all looked in great condition, and they'd all enjoyed success in some form in their own competitions. He asked me to go along to his nutrition shop and he wanted to know what I could do in terms of cardio training, as he'd never helped an amputee before. Unlike nowadays, there were very few of us competing at that time. I researched and researched, looking for amputees who competed in bodybuilding, and it wasn't a long list. He wrote me a training programme and a diet plan, he helped me with practicing the poses, putting together a routine, and he gave up a lot of his time to help me. I wanted to repay that by sticking to everything by the letter.

I wasn't doing it for money, I just wanted a purpose and I wanted to make my wife and sons proud. I wanted them to speak of me in present tense, proud of what I was doing now and not just what I'd done as a soldier. Natalie could see I had that passion back, and she supported me all the way. Week by week, I'd visit Tommo, he'd take a look at my physique and give me a very honest assessment of where I needed to put in more effort, where I needed to adjust my calorie intake, my water intake, my cardio. I was hungry almost constantly, it had taken over my life but in a positive way. I lived to his letter, existing on turkey breasts, broccoli and rice, and out each morning before breakfast on my crutches with a bin bag and a few layers on, sweating for an hour before anyone else in the house was even stirring.

As an amputee, I couldn't just go out running, so I had to improvise. I found myself on the children's trampoline with them, jumping in a sauna suit and covering the boys in sweat. I went out walking on my crutches but, in getting caught up in the preparation, I overlooked that I was losing body fat from everywhere, including my leg. This meant I needed more than one new socket fitting for my leg stump in the build-up to competing. No longer at Headley Court and no longer serving, I couldn't use the limb fitting department there, so I was now under the NHS, a patient at Luton and Dunstable limb fitting centre, and was posing them problems instead.

It was a world apart from the level I'd become accustomed to, not in terms of the prosthetists, as they were and continue to be brilliant – they had all the time in the world for me and my needs and ambitions. But at Headley, I'd head down to prosthetics and there would be music, four or five blokes I knew well, and the time would pass quickly and often with plenty of laughs. Luton was a quiet, bland room, with many of the patients in their later years and many with little or no motivation or desire to walk again. It was an eye opener, and sad to see just how different my early experiences of becoming an amputee had clearly been to theirs – surrounded by positivity and hard work and routine and access to every type of professional the MOD could offer. Having had the chance, while sat in the waiting rooms, to talk with several of the people who attended Luton, most were amputees as a result of diabetes, cancer or road traffic accidents, and they were openly envious of the level of care the military amputees received – and understandably so.

As the weeks turned into months and as I became increasingly hungry and fatigued, I'd take myself out of the house while the family enjoyed a takeaway and not come home until they'd finished. There were days where I would really struggle with the low carbs and low calories, to the point where I'd dig to the back of the children's treat cupboard and find an old chocolate bar, even if it was out of date, devour it, hide the wrapper at the back of the cupboard and hope no one would find out. I'd walk around the rest of that day with a guilty look on my face, convinced my wife knew I'd sunk low enough to eat out-of-date children's chocolate. The reality was, Natalie wasn't fussed, but I had an overwhelming fear of letting her down. In hindsight, it was an unhealthy mentality to have developed, but having a deadline to this diet meant I put more pressure on myself than anyone else could. I was my own biggest critic and I often overlooked the parts of my appearance that would help me do well on stage and focused on where I needed to improve, although the moments of binge eating probably weren't going to help.

I'd been tired in the army, to the point of hallucinating at times, but this hunger thing was a new challenge. I found the weight training enjoyable and I loved seeing the weekly differences in my appearance. As the diet became tougher, the training sessions became more tiring and the plates on the bars were getting lighter yet feeling heavier. This was a new kind of mental toughness, but I knew if I put in the effort now and trusted Tommo's process, the final outcome would be one I could look back on with pride.

As the competition neared, I needed to pick a track to carry out my posing routine to. I wanted something uplifting both for myself and the crowd. At that time, I thought this would be like the experience of running on a blade – get it out of my system and move on, so I wanted to enjoy every second up there. I chose AC/DC's 'Shoot to Thrill' and set about putting together a posing routine, a chance to show off my best features. The effort and physical strain of posing was something not to be underestimated. Tensing each muscle for a prolonged period under the spotlights while dehydrated, and trying to out-pose others on stage while not cramping up, was a challenge I hadn't appreciated until it came to really doing it.

Competition week saw me stepping into the unknown. My carbohydrates gradually increased in the days leading up to competing, my water intake also went up a lot, as did my salt intake (known as sodium loading). Having eaten such bland food for months, the amount of salt now on my food wasn't exactly pleasant. It was all part of the process and I had every faith that Tommo and my own self-discipline had gotten me to the best possible condition I could have been in, for an amputee and for someone who'd never done this before – for someone who, three years earlier, had almost died and looked very ill and underweight. This would help to bring closure to that chapter in my mind – to embrace it and move forward positively as a person with a disability.

As for the approach to the diet in that final week, the salt was meant to help draw the water out from under the skin, creating a tighter look and making the skin almost like tracing paper. The increase in carbohydrates helped to fill my muscles, now quite depleted from the prolonged dieting, and helped bring out that vascular look. With muscles being over 70% water, the water loading would help fill them, drawing water away from elsewhere and helping to increase the appearance of separation.

We drove down to Margate the night before the competition and checked into our hotel. I had an appointment booked in with the show's tanning company. This was a whole new experience and the first time I was around bodybuilders and the people I'd be competing with. The feeling was an uncomfortable one, stripped down to nothing but a sock covering my genitals and feeling like the smallest man in the room in more ways than one. I posed a challenge to the ladies who were spray tanning me, as I couldn't keep my prosthetic leg on and so I needed to stand balanced on one leg for almost ten minutes. I was sprayed from all different angles in all different places, and had to remain stood in front of a big fan while the tan dried off. I was a dark mahogany colour, and they said it would get darker overnight and it would cover the hotel bed sheets – and Natalie, if I attempted to get a bit frisky with her that night. The reason for being so dark was that the stage lighting would be very bright and, if we weren't dark enough, any definition we had wouldn't be seen on stage, so there was method to it. I felt uncomfortable and a bit irritable with the tan and wearing the loosest clothes possible to avoid any of it coming off.

It was at that point that I began to think I'd made a mistake. I went from nervous excitement to self-doubt. These blokes in the other categories had an aura about them, but also an arrogance, and not one that I personally admired. I could tell early on that these people were not my cup of tea. First impressions count, and the overwhelming feeling was that many of them thought very highly of themselves. I was also extremely thirsty, as my body had taken on so much water all week and now it had been shunted to the opposite extreme. My water was cut at 18:00, and I couldn't take on anymore until after my time on stage was done. This process would lead to my body getting rid of all the liquid I'd taken on all week, and I was up every twenty minutes throughout the night, pissing.

It's amazing how much you want water when you can't have it.

One perk was that I could enjoy a fatty meal that night at the hotel – a mixed grill! I was also allowed to accompany this with a glass of red wine, and that was my first mistake. I ended up enjoying more than one glass, as the reality and the nerves well and truly hit me and the other competitors made me question my own physique. It was at this meal that I met a couple of the lads who were in the disability class with me, and I wasn't prepared for it, to be honest. I was more than used to being around amputees and seeing lads looking their worst, but I'd never really been in the company of people who were born with disabilities or suffered different types of life changing injuries.

The lads I met had cerebral palsy. My knowledge of the condition wasn't great at that time but, in a naïve way, I sympathised with them and took stock of how lucky I was to grow up as a perfectly healthy boy. School can be a cruel place, as I found out, but I realised on meeting these lads that they'd come through a lot more than I did as youngsters. I was in awe of their outlook and how hard they'd clearly worked. It was certainly a new learning curve.

I couldn't really sleep that night. Needing to piss, nerves and dreaming of a glass of water meant my mind was in overdrive. We went down to breakfast where, again, I could eat a good meal, with no fluids. Then it was off to the theatre where the competition would be held. Admittedly, the dehydration had done its magic during the night and I was happy that I'd got to this point. If nothing else, I'd come a long way from where I was in hospital and I'd stuck to my word that I'd compete in a bodybuilding competition. Natalie couldn't really hug me, although I'm not sure I had any tan left on me, looking at the state of the bedding. But her saying that she was proud of me, and a video message from my boys wishing me luck, made me feel like a king.

Then I had a few sips of whiskey for Dutch courage and off we went.

A meeting was first on the list, with all the athletes coming together in the theatre to be told of the running order of the categories. It was a chance to step on stage and familiarise myself with the markings where I'd need to stand. I then made my way backstage, which resembled a cattle market – twenty or so bodybuilders squeezed into a small theatre dressing room for one, with a couple of weights to warm up with which were like gold dust to get your hands on. I was watching the experienced ones, seeing what they'd brought along. Some had resistance bands and Haribo, Coca Cola or Lucozade (the glucose, in small amounts around twenty minutes before stepping on stage, helped with vascularity). Some tried to find a place to sleep, to speed time up, and I imagined they were all as thirsty and irritable as me.

Some were helpful and some were full of questions about my leg. Then one particular bloke walked in, made a big space for himself and his kit, took to slagging a few people off and criticising their physiques and was just a general bell-end. It seemed he was playing mind games, and it worked, as a few heads dropped. I was amazed that he wasn't given a slap or two for his insolence!

The disability class was the first category up. There were three of us – myself, a lad called Josh and a lad called Dan, both with cerebral palsy and both having competed in bodybuilding before. In fact, when I'd done all the research on disability bodybuilding, these two lads were the ones who'd appeared in my searches, and I felt privileged to be stood side by side with them. We walked out in single file, before taking up the relaxed pose on our spots on the marked-out stage. The lights were intense, hot and bright, but the brightness helped to blur out just how many people were in the crowd watching – the theatre was a sell-out.

I could hear the odd scream of encouragement as we turned a quarter to our right. My smile covered my face from ear to ear, and the hairs on the back of my neck couldn't stand any more on end. It was such an adrenaline rush, my heart felt like it was about to explode out of my chest. There was a quarter turn to the right to face the rear of the stage and we were asked to adopt the lat spread pose, followed by the rear double bicep. The practicing had definitely helped to familiarise me with how the poses should feel when done correctly as, with no mirrors on stage, I was feeling the tension throughout my body. In the momentary lulls while the judges were marking us, all I could think of was "I hope my penis doesn't look small in these posing trunks!"

Another two quarter turns and a side chest and side triceps pose, and it was all done – it seemed to have gone by in a flash. The judges were looking for symmetry, which was obviously not going to be my strongest point, given the lack of one leg! They were also looking for conditioning, how dry our skin was, muscle mass, stage presence, definition and proportion – legs in proportion to upper body. That was something I didn't want to be picked up on, so I put in plenty of hours to ensure my left leg was thickset, if not defined.

The three of us left the stage once the judges were happy, and we then came back on as individuals to go through our posing routines. It was a chance to show off our strongest poses to the track of our choice for ninety seconds. I included a couple of Arnold Schwarzenegger's classic poses, although I don't think I did them the same justice he did.

I was first out, and the MC read a backstory on me – the fact that I was a veteran led to a standing ovation, and I could barely hear my track playing. It was overwhelming in every positive way you could imagine. The feeling was euphoric and, as I carried out my poses, I was already thinking: "I want to do this again."

I finished my routine, looked for Natalie, blew her a kiss, waved and walked off – well, more floated off. My face ached more than my body with all the smiling, and now I'd done my routine, I couldn't wait to find myself a bottle of water. I was already dreaming of the feast of a meal I was going to demolish afterwards! I stood backstage to watch Josh's and Dan's routines, and all three of us had a great response from the crowd.

Once the individual routines were completed, the judges called us back onto the stage for our placings. At that point, the enjoyment, the closure on losing my leg and the confidence I'd gained from those few minutes were better than any placing. But, as they were read in reverse order, I heard my name called out as the winner of the disability class, in what felt like an out-of-body experience. That moment, those words, opened so many doors and paved the way for all that would follow in the coming years. Pure Elite, through embracing a disability class, had done more for me than I could thank them for.

I was presented with my trophy, and no sooner had I gone backstage to get dressed (I was never one for standing around in just the trunks), my phone was already going mad. A friend had filmed and uploaded my routine and the results onto social media, and it was through the power of the more positive aspect of that forum that I'd be offered an opportunity I couldn't have been more enthusiastic about.

We made our way home, with me in the passenger seat and in a little bit of a food coma, replying to all the messages from friends. I'd been warned of the post-competition blues that might follow. A lot of bodybuilders suffer with a dramatic comedown after such a high

– the empty feeling of returning to normality. But I didn't have time to experience that dip, as my video was seen by Lee Thompson, the head of the NPC (National Physique Committee) in America. He was inviting me over to Houston, Texas, to compete in their disability class in March 2015 at the Phil Heath Classic. After realising he was deadly serious, I jumped at the chance.

In my mind, competing in the US would be a step up in class, so I knew I had to improve on how I looked in Margate. Having seen the photographs from that day, there was plenty of room for improvement and I was keen to pick the brains of more than one bodybuilder for this competition. I took a couple of weeks rest from training and dieting and enjoyed the rebound effect that came with eating high calories off the back of such strict dieting. My body felt like a sponge, soaking up every unhealthy calorie I consumed. It had been depleted for so many months that it felt like my sense of taste and smell had heightened. It was good to relax, for my mind to switch off, and to enjoy family meals and quality time at home, knowing that I'd soon be putting myself through competition preparation again.

It was nice to step back into Atlas fresh from competing, and the main question my friends in there asked was "what's next?". So I couldn't wait to tell them I was off to the States for my next competition. Just a few weeks prior to Pure Elite, I thought it would be a one-off thing, but having felt the euphoria that accompanied my time on stage, I was glad I'd get to do it all again.

With Christmas out of the way, I was in a much better starting place than I was when I first asked Tommo to help me. With his own commitments, he wasn't really in a position to dedicate that same time for this competition, but recommended another highly respected bodybuilder and trainer, Mark Etherden. His knowledge was fascinating and his expectations, with his own reputation to uphold, were the step up I needed to compete in America. He took a look at my photos from Margate but wanted me to be much leaner. I was excited at the thought of building on what Tommo had helped me create, but was well aware of the toll this would take on my body.

I saw Mark weekly, driving down to Hockliffe to his supplement store, where I'd strip down to my pants in the middle of the shop and he'd weigh me and critique me. His photos and trophies that decorated the walls were motivation enough to make me, once again, trust the process. I was almost a complete novice in this sport, the likes of Tommo and Mark were not, and I felt privileged to have been able to pick the brains of two highly regarded bodybuilders.

This new preparation demanded even more discipline from me. I'd enjoyed the few weeks of living my version of "Man v Food" and my body did not enjoy going back to those dark, lonely places that needed to be embraced in order to better myself. I'd often be so fatigued during this preparation that, on more than one occasion, I'd pull into bays at the side of the road to sleep. The improvements were clear to see and that kept me pushing on, although it had friends questioning if this sort of punishment was worth it, to give up socialising, drinking, good food and all the things I enjoyed in the army. But that deadline in front of me felt like it was giving me the structure I needed.

I flew out to Houston three days before the competition to allow for adjustment to the time difference. I'd also been advised that the body retains water on long flights and I'd need a few days to settle down and get rid of the added fluid, which wouldn't be a problem in the Texas heat. I found some great gyms to train at in those couple of days and met some brilliant people. To this day, any Americans I've met in bodybuilding and Strongman have been great. One thing I had to resist before competing, though, were all the amazing American restaurants.

I knew a bit more of what to expect with the briefings and tanning and the dehydration, and felt better prepared all round. I'd improved tenfold in my physique and couldn't wait to meet the people I'd be sharing the stage with. I was massively disappointed to find out the night before, at the athlete registration, that the other disabled bodybuilders hadn't turned up and so I'd be competing alone. I'd really wanted to see how I'd fare against them, and I'd put in so much effort for a moment it all felt like a waste – until I phoned Natalie from the hotel. She told me to flip it on its head and see it as a positive. That time on stage would be mine to leave a good impression and to come away with no regrets – she always had a way with finding the words to remind me how much I'd put in. I was aware that we hadn't spent much quality time together as I'd become more reclusive in my pursuit to improve, so it needed to be worth it.

I'd booked my hotel opposite the arena and could see the queue of spectators building up outside – it went all the way around the building, and I began to realise how big the sport was in America. I made my way across, walking past the crowds with a competitor pass around my neck and even darker than I'd been at Pure Elite. I handed my CD to the DJ on arriving and I'd wanted something very English for my routine – 'Morning Glory' by Oasis was the song of choice.

Backstage was much more spacious this time and the organisers had left out plenty of weights. There seemed to be more humility and everyone seemed friendly, although most people thought I was Australian. I think they expected an Englishman to talk like someone off the set of Downton Abbey. I had time to talk with Lee, the organiser, who'd kindly invited me over and made this experience a reality. Lee's one of the nicest people I met in bodybuilding, and I was glad I got the chance to thank him. He told me they had a surprise for me later in the day and that I wouldn't be disappointed with the lack of competition in my category. This occupied my thoughts as I lay on the floor, fully dressed until the last possible moment as I was surrounded by men who looked like they'd been chiselled from granite. I could hear the crowds making their way in and the sound system playing music to pass the time before the show started. The noise was on par with a festival – it was deafening. Again, just as in Margate, disability would be up first.

I heard my backstory being read out – "All the way from England, Mark Smith." I stepped out from behind the curtain to take my place on stage, and the sight was amazing. Over four thousand people had filled the arena and were on their feet as I made my way to the X on stage. Even the four judges were up on their feet and, for that brief moment, I felt gutted that I was there on my own – that Natalie wasn't one of those faces in the crowd. But I wanted to do her, my boys, Atlas, Mark and Tommo proud. I'd worked even harder on my posing, having much more appreciation for how draining it is, and felt great.

Unlike with Pure Elite, this part of the competition was the pre-judging and I was free to head back to the hotel for a few hours before the finals in the evening. Still conscious that I had to step back on stage, I had a small meal and a few sips of water and slept to make the time go quicker, but not before phoning Natalie to tell her of the response I got and the conversation I had with Lee.

The evening was an equally incredible, electrifying atmosphere – all the more so because Phil Heath would be doing a guest pose in the interval. 99% of that crowd were undoubtedly there to witness one of the most successful bodybuilders ever, posing up on stage. I performed my routine and accepted my trophy, but as I made my way off the stage, the security guard called me to one side and told me to wait. I wondered what I'd done wrong. Then the lights went down, the volume of the music went up a notch or ten and the crowd cheered. Enter Phil Heath. He made his way through the crowd like a boxer in their ring walk and stepped up on stage. There were photos being taken everywhere and I felt excited to be stood so close to see him posing. I'd said to Natalie on the phone, imagine if I get the chance to meet him.

His routine took the roof off, it made mine look shit. Then, Bob Chicherillo interviewed him on stage, while I was still stood next to this security guard. I was listening to him interview Phil Heath, when I heard him mention that they had someone very special fly over all the way from England and they should invite him up on stage. I was pretty sure I was the only Englishman in that arena, and my mouth became as dry as the Sahara Desert. Phil Heath took the microphone and invited me to join him on stage and asked if I'd like to have a pose down with him right there. I felt like a boy stood next to a man but jumped at the chance. He was phenomenal, both as a bodybuilder and as a person, and those few minutes will be something I'll never forget.

Lee Thompson wasn't wrong when he said they had something special planned for me. But I never thought I'd be stood next to one of the sport's most successful ever bodybuilders and for him to know me by name. I can never thank them both enough for allowing me that moment. It's genuinely one of those experiences that will stay with me forever and one that I'll be boring the grandchildren with one day. It was a moment that has sort of defined me since. In the gym I'm still "that guy who was on stage with Phil Heath" – something most people in the sport will never get the opportunity to experience.

Prior to that, I'd been the bloke in the corner backstage, head down and tracksuit on to hide my inferior physique. Heading back into that same room afterwards was a different experience entirely. On leaving the arena, I could hear the same words over and over: "That's the guy who was just on stage with Phil Heath", and I felt ten foot tall. I'd been eyeing up a Hard Rock restaurant next to the arena from the moment I checked in, and I made my way straight there after the event. I ate in, then took an extra couple of meals back in doggy bags and passed out in a food coma on my hotel bed, with chocolate cake on my chest and face.

Breakfast the next morning was the same story, the "all you can eat buffet" meant I asked for a table for four just for myself and filled it with plates and plates of food. I'm sure that, if we'd been asked to step back on stage that evening, they'd have asked who the bloated mess in the disability class was. It was my first time in the States and I wanted to savour at least some of the local cuisine before flying home.

I made my way to the airport and it seemed my luck was still on the up, as the British Airways lady at the check-in desk upgraded me to first class for free. It was clear to everyone during boarding that this was an alien experience for me, as I broke the partition between me and the man opposite and I was still half-covered in the layers upon layers of fake tan that I couldn't scrub off. I was still a shade more appropriate to a garden fence than a person. The seat went all the way back to a bed, and I was able to sleep the whole flight home because the food coma hadn't fully worn off.

After landing, it was surreal from the offset. My phone went ballistic with sponsorship offers, messages of congratulations and offers for documentaries and magazine interviews. I took the view that this moment would soon pass and I'd be old news. But I decided to embrace the interest – if nothing else, maybe it would help promote getting veterans and people with disabilities into sport. If someone who'd looked so ill and weak in hospital could get to this point, then anyone could. Despite initially intending to only compete once to see if I could, I now found myself with invites to more competitions in the UK. The frequency would take its toll; most bodybuilders advised me that they only really competed once or twice a year, due to how much it drains the body and, perhaps more importantly, the mind.

I went on to compete eight times in 2015, between March and October, and I certainly found those experienced bodybuilders were right. I felt exhausted, and I had to restrict my body of good food and relaxation for so long that what started off as an amazing experience became something I resented. I wanted to play my part in helping develop disability bodybuilding, and I enjoyed the rewards that came with that, as numbers began to grow on stage with each competition. But at the end of competing for that year, I welcomed the break from dieting and decided I'd only compete once or twice in 2016. Other opportunities, however, would lead to new challenges altogether.

I look back on bodybuilding fondly. Those feelings of hunger and tiredness were massively outweighed by the pride of stepping on stage and the confidence it gave me to walk proud as an amputee. I had no shame in my appearance and I stepped onto stages I never would have thought possible. I competed in able-bodied classes to test myself. I competed in Atlas's own bodybuilding show, which was amazing, more so that I was able to win the disability class in a show in my hometown with friends and family filling the seats. I guest posed on a pro stage, having been invited on the IFBB Pro Show at Body Power, which really excited me. I'd walked around the NEC Arena two years before with friends, in awe of all the athletes there. To compete on such a big platform was surreal.

I appeared in Muscle & Fitness, Men's Health and Flex and Train magazines as a result of these shows and the positive name I managed to make for myself. I felt like I'd absolutely made the right decision by opting not to stay and work at Bannatynes, but to follow the urge to find a purpose and to discover if I had more to give. With the mindset that I wanted to be someone my children would be proud of, I felt I'd justified pursuing another avenue.

The Phil Heath Classic, Houston, Texas, 2015: Stood side by side with one of the most successful bodybuilders ever to step on stage. Something that I'll be proudly telling the grandchildren about!

Airfield Anarchy: My first physical challenge after losing my leg, a 5km mud obstacle course, raising money for Blesma

13

STRENGTH

enjoyed some rest after the eight bodybuilding competitions that
occupied much of my time in 2015. I had a really positive outlook
on 2016, and a resurgence in looking forward to stepping on stage.
I prepared for my first bodybuilding show of that year and felt much
stronger with a relaxed diet over the winter, so I believed I'd do well on
stage. That was until I had my head turned, although I was reluctant
to embrace the idea at first. Britain's first Disabled Strongman, Gary
Clarke, contacted me. He was someone I had a lot of time and respect
for, in his relentless dedication to growing Disabled Strongman as a
legitimate competition.

We'd followed each other online, through our respective sports, in
the previous couple of years. He asked if I was free for a phone call and
explained that he was organising a training day in Kent, to encourage
new people to try Disabled Strongman. I was a little hesitant at first,
as I was still very much in that Headley Court mentality – I have a
prosthetic leg and, therefore, I don't need to compete in a sport that
would require me to sit in a wheelchair. I didn't think I'd be any good
at it, to be honest.

I grew up watching the *World's Strongest Man* on television every
Christmas and I loved it. I loved watching seemingly superhuman men
do the almost impossible – from pulling trains, planes and trucks to

deadlifting cars. It's the alpha male of all sports, no voting from judges on who looks the best, but a simple black-and-white competition where the strongest man wins. That side of it massively appealed to me and, after talking it through with Natalie, I agreed to go along to the open day.

They were lifting atlas stones, pressing logs and pulling sleds. I stayed at the back, reserved and almost fearing to embarrass myself. I'd gained enough confidence through bodybuilding to not be worried by the appearance of my leg, but I certainly didn't consider myself strong enough to compete in a sport like this.

The blokes were a great bunch, though, offering tips and encouragement. I was pretty much last to try everything, as I watched other people have a go first. I'd never touched most of this stuff before and it wasn't equipment you'd find lying about in a normal gym. Sitting in the wheelchair, as the tray to protect my lap was clipped into place and a giant of a man stood behind to avoid it tipping backwards, I had my first go at lifting an atlas stone. I picked it up from the oil barrel on my left side, rolled it up onto my chest and across, with a twist of my mid-section, onto the barrel to my right. It felt natural, and having long arms helped. Going last meant I'd watched the technique and it went smoothly, so the people running the day asked if I wanted to try a heavier atlas stone. I was now enjoying the experience and completely understood the need to do this in a wheelchair, so I couldn't wait to try the next stone, which went across even easier. In total, I went up four weights, lifting a 100kg atlas stone on my first day ever having a go. This was a weight that hadn't even been used at the previous World's Strongest Disabled Man and it meant I'd made a good impression. Then Gary asked me to compete in Britain's Strongest Disabled Man, which was only six weeks away.

I couldn't wait to phone Natalie to tell her what an amazing day I had. In my mind, I'd already pulled out of the bodybuilding competition I was due to compete in that year. I knew coming away from bodybuilding meant I wouldn't have to diet or worry how I looked, which appealed to me. I watched video upon video of Disabled Strongman events online over the next few days and started to look for suitable gyms close by that would let a one-legged bloke train there. I couldn't wait to get stuck in, both to the added calories that my body would need and to practicing the events. The days flew by and I was wishing there was more time for me to train as much as possible. I threw myself into it 100%, just as I had with my first bodybuilding competition. Unlike that, however, I didn't have brains to pick, as it wasn't a sport many people from Atlas Gym competed in.

It was trial and error, really, and I used the "Britains" as an eye opener, to watch and learn. In the last few days before the competition, there was no need to dehydrate or add loads of salt to food or cover the bed in fake tan, so I felt a lot more relaxed and kept my expectations realistic. As with stepping into bodybuilding, I was a complete novice, but I decided to give every ounce of effort I had. I was joined that week by a couple of people from Channel 4 who'd initially got in contact, wanting to do a short film on bodybuilding. They seemed equally interested in covering this new venture, and I think I surprised them as much as myself – everyone else – on the day. I mean, I told them and my family that I'd be ecstatic to be in the top ten at the end of the competition.

These were Britain's best disabled strongmen and the numbers were far greater than in bodybuilding, with twenty-three contestants, including myself, competing. It was a big event, and qualifying places for the World's Strongest Disabled Man were at stake. I hadn't paid much attention to that, as I believed it was way out of my reach at that stage. I mainly just wanted to enjoy the competition and the fact that I could eat what I liked and drink water whenever I wanted. I think my previous experience in bodybuilding made me enjoy the whole Strongman scene even more.

I arrived in Kent to see some faces I'd met at the training day and some faces I hadn't. Some were really big blokes – broad shoulders and backs and forearms like Popeye. My eyes were drawn to two lads I thought I should watch for the day. Everything about them just looked professional and their appearance emanated strength in abundance. One of them – Greg Bramwell – would become a good friend. He had the Viking beard to match the build and I thought, during warming up, "I won't go far wrong if I watch him."

He'd followed what I'd been doing in Strongman and we spent the day together talking. He had my dry sense of humour and gave me plenty of advice for each event. He added to the whole experience for me, as did as two other top men, Tony Butcher and Dan Piggott. It was a much more social atmosphere with these lads, a far cry from the hood up, headphones on atmosphere that I'd experienced at a couple of bodybuilding shows – although it has to be said, not with anyone from the disability class. There seemed to be a togetherness with people with disabilities that separated them in a really positive way from some of the more self-confident pretty boys, and I was drawn to that non-egotistical collective.

The first event was an iconic feature of Strongman and one I couldn't wait to have a go at – the truck pull. Being in a seated class meant I was in a category comprised of people with lower limb deficiencies, from paralysis to cerebral palsy, spina bifida and above-knee amputations like myself. So our category's truck pull was done arm over arm, sat on the floor facing the truck, with twenty-five metres of rope in front of us and a wooden block to press our feet against. Being the first event, it was done in alphabetical order, so I was one of the last to go. It was beautiful weather, and I enjoyed watching and taking in the atmosphere, one of the standout things that attracted me.

My boys were off playing when Natalie went to tell them I was up soon. At that point, the weather turned and it began raining, which made gripping the rope tougher. I walked up to the area and sat on the floor so that I could have the harness attached to my upper body. At that point I looked to my right and my sons surprised me with banners they'd made, saying "Come on Daddy" and they were cheering me on. So much pride filled me at that moment that it sort of became like an out-of-body experience – I felt like I could pull an aeroplane. This was the only event they really wanted to watch, and as I heard "athlete ready, take the strain" and then the whistle, I pulled like their lives depended on it, like a man possessed. I put my head down and focused only on my hands and the rope. It was my thinking that looking at the truck would be disheartening, as it would appear to not be moving as fast as I wanted it to or even getting any closer. I thought if I looked down, kept fast hands and pulled non-stop until I heard the whistle, it would be fine.

In fact, it was better than fine – here I was at my first ever Strongman competition, in the rain, having never pulled a truck, with my boys cheering me on, and I'd only gone and won the truck pull! I'd gone from the new bloke who nobody knew on the athletes list, to sitting top of the leader board after the first event. To win such an iconic event almost brought a tear to my eye and I was grinning from ear to ear. I wasn't there to win it, just to learn, to enjoy the day and show my boys that I could pull a truck. I still didn't believe that I could go on to win the entire competition, just that I'd had a good start and my hopes of finishing top ten were looking like a real possibility.

The next couple of events weren't great for me – the log press and the axe hold. Both required a lot of deltoid strength and stability, something that the gunshot to my shoulder definitely hindered. I pressed until that side of my body gave way and held the axe aloft until my shoulder could shake no more. It put me back in a humbler position, and my feeling was that I'd just had a lucky start.

Endurance plays a big part in Strongman. The ability to switch the adrenaline on and off and be able to give 100% for every single event was hard going, and it looked like I'd given it all in the truck pull. It got late and Natalie had to take the boys home before the final three events – the Hercules hold, the car deadlift and the famous atlas stones. I wanted to get the two I knew I wouldn't excel at out of the way and was keen to finish on a high. I was asking for tips for the Hercules hold, and one of the lads suggested wrapping my lifting straps tight around my wrists while making a clenched fist until just before I was due up. The feeling was one of cramp and pins and needles, but this event was a test of grip strength, which, as it turned out, was a strong point of mine.

The event consisted of sitting in a wheelchair between two railway sleepers, each weighing 80kg, holding them using the handles at the end of chains attached to the sleepers. I noticed some lads weren't sat centrally between the sleepers and, as soon as they took the full weight, were pulled to the side they were closer to, so the other hand let go of the handle. Some lads struggled to hold on for sixty seconds. I removed my wrist straps and could barely open my hands, but I was meticulous in making sure the chair was central. I closed my eyes, relaxed into the chair and took the strain, before the spotters let go of the sleepers. The whistle went and the timer started. I felt the jolt of the sleepers as their full weight pulled my arms apart. I slowed my breathing down and shut everything out – I'd found a zen. The time elapsed was called out every thirty seconds by the head referee, a man I was desperate to impress, as I'd grown up watching him and he was something of a living legend in Strongman – Magnus ver Magnusson!

The lead at that point was just over a minute, and as I went beyond the two-minute mark, the crowd really started to get behind me, cheering me on to keep holding. It was strange; I felt comfortable, convinced people were holding the sleepers, but not wanting to open my eyes to check in case I lost my concentration. With three lads still to go after me, I knew I had to hold until my grip gave way. I didn't want to concede points if I could keep going. I held those sleepers for four minutes and one second, a record in Disabled Strongman. I opened my eyes and smiled to be greeted by cheers and claps of approval from spectators and athletes alike. It was amazing. I went on to win that event by over two-and-a-half clear minutes. I phoned Natalie and she was disappointed they had to leave when they did.

Winning that event gave me the benefit of going last on the car deadlift. I was excited about this event, the thought of deadlifting a car was true strength. Some of the lads were phenomenal lifters and I enjoyed watching them. I was in admiration and awe the whole day, to be honest, and seeing men with serious disabilities carrying out feats of strength that the average human being with full use of all their limbs would struggle to do, certainly gave me an extra boost when it came to exercising my strength on the day. The car to be deadlifted was an old Fiat Pinto and the rear wheels had to fully clear the ground on each lift in order for it to be given the down signal by the referee and counted as a repetition. I won this event by no more than a couple of repetitions and now found myself top of the leader board, heading into the final event, the atlas stones. I knew that if I was able to lift all five, then I'd done enough to become Britain's Strongest Disabled Man.

I loved the atlas stones and they would go on to be, without doubt, my strongest event in the sport. My turn came and all five stones went up and, for 2016 at least, I knew I was the strongest disabled man in the whole of Great Britain, something that still doesn't really sink in. Natalie had encouraged me to go down and give it a go on that training day, and now my dad was watching me in the lead and I could see him beaming with pride. I knew I'd done him proud time and again, but the boy in me always sought his approval and recognition. We hugged and I covered his top in the tacky (a sticky sap-like glue to help with grip on the atlas stones) Dan had kindly shared with me. That was something which left a real positive impression and was a credit to those blokes' temperaments on the day – we were all competing together, and yet everyone was more than happy to offer kit, chalk, tacky, food and advice, and I've never forgotten the ones who were good men.

The placings were called out in reverse order and with just me and Greg left, I felt I'd chosen well when I watched him, picking up tips from his technique throughout the day. We'd battled it out and laughed and encouraged each other all day, it was brilliant, and there was mutual respect as we both acknowledged how hard we'd had to work to be in this position. Being called up as Britain's Strongest Disabled Man, walking up to collect the trophy and knowing I'd be going up against the best in the world in a few months was surreal. I phoned Natalie before driving home and she was in tears. I couldn't wait to show my boys the trophy in the morning, and for them to be able to go into school and say their dad was Britain's Strongest Disabled Man.

I went into that competition wanting to learn and I'd certainly done that. There were a lot more pointers to take away, including using things like tacky, sleeves, belts and chalks, all things I invested in the very next day. Things I needed sooner than I thought, as I was going to be off to the World's Strongest Disabled Man in a few months to represent Great Britain. That sent tingles down my spine! I'd told the people from Channel 4 that I'd like to try and qualify for the "Worlds" in around three years' time.

It had come much earlier than I thought!

In preparation for the "Worlds", I put myself forward at the annual Grenadier Day, a coming together of past and present Grenadier Guards in an enjoyable reunion and family outing, to pull two army Land Rovers at the same time in front of all in attendance. I was proud to be a Grenadier and proud that I could attend Grenadier Day as Britain's Strongest Disabled Man. I wanted to combine the two, while also giving something back. So, with Prince Phillip in attendance (who asked if I would be pulling the Land Rovers with my teeth!), I pulled both vehicles to raise money for the Colonel's Fund, our regimental charity that supports injured Grenadiers, their families and the families of Grenadiers we have sadly lost.

But I couldn't really enjoy the day because I was so nervous. People said they were hanging around waiting to see me pull the vehicles, and comments that I wouldn't be able to do it were heard. Rob Creighton, another former Grenadier and a man who has put himself out to help me time and again, was by my side to feed the rope through. Unlike "Britains", my warm-up consisted of a couple of slaps on the back! The noise of support was deafening, but above it all I could hear my boys' voices screaming, "Come on Daddy!" And away we went, pulling the Land Rovers twenty-five metres and raising over £1,000 for a cause that has helped myself and friends of mine time and time again.

It was a huge confidence boost ahead of the "Worlds" and a small gesture to say, "thank you".

As I said, I used the time before the "Worlds" to invest in a lot more kit, to enable me to practice more specific events, but my feelgood bubble was soon to be well and truly burst. You remember I mentioned Woody and Spence in Chapter 9 – the two lads who kept me alive until the helicopter arrived, after the shooting in Canada? Well Spence, Spencer Beynon, a sergeant in the Royal Welsh Regiment, became one of my biggest supporters. He was a man I owed my life to and one I had the greatest of love and respect for. Spence loved Strongman; I spoke to him in the days that followed the competition, and he told me how proud he was of me. He was struggling with post-traumatic stress disorder, which had led to his medical discharge from the army. He explained to me that I was the first lad he'd treated who'd gone on to live, and it seemed it raised a lot of upsetting memories of friends he'd lost in Iraq and Afghanistan.

Being from different regiments, I had to find him on social media to get in contact originally. I wanted so much to thank him for all he'd given me, and I sent him a message with my phone number. He called me almost immediately and drove from Llanelli in Wales to Milton Keynes to see me. It took him around four hours, and it was late when he arrived. As I heard his car pull up, I made my way outside and we stood hugging in the street, crying for a good few minutes. We'd speak, then hug again, and I thanked him and thanked him and invited him in to meet Natalie and Ellis. We sat up all night talking, and it was clear we'd both been asking people from our respective regiments about putting us in touch for some time.

After that, we spent hour upon hour on the phone and he seemed to be doing well with charity work and had got back into his mixed martial arts. Physically, he was as tough as they come – his dad had been a Welsh Guard, so he grew up with a military mindset from a young age – but mentally, I wasn't sure how he truly was. He would be so keen to hear what I was doing that he didn't really want to talk about how he was getting on. Although we hadn't served together before Canada, my injury had forged an instant bond between us, and maybe it was karma or kismet or something.

It was Spence who'd taken the time to help me settle into working as one of the safety staff on the ranges in Canada. If you remember, I told you how I didn't feel like I could ask the officer in charge of the ranges any questions and I wanted to be as knowledgeable as possible, ironically, before starting with live ammunition. As I said, Spence was the only person happy to answer all my queries, and he actually praised me for being so inquisitive. Being slightly older than me, he was someone I looked up to. He was a highly competent soldier and a natural leader, and every phone call built me up to feeling ten foot tall.

To hear that his struggles had led to his death broke my heart. I cried and cried almost continuously for days. I wished he'd opened up to me about his struggles, so I could have gone just a tiny way to repaying all he'd done for me. I would have driven to Llanelli in a heartbeat to support him, my whole family owed him a debt of gratitude for his actions the day I was shot. I would have done anything for that man, and I feel honoured to have been in his presence. I was equally honoured to get the opportunity to stand and talk at his funeral. His family were wonderful, and it was clear where he had developed his resilience and strength and wonderful loud Welsh accent.

After the funeral, I listened to stories from lads who were in his regiment and stories from his family. I felt so much pride in him, but so much grief that such a great man wasn't still with us, and wondering if it could have been prevented made the pain worse. I was so broken up about his death that I chose, wrongly, to lock it away – I didn't know how else to deal with it. Our regiment had lost lads on previous tours, and each time it hit us hard. This felt different, though. It felt like a member of my own family was gone and had left a great hole in my life. So I buried it. I chose to put it to the back of my mind, because thinking about him would bring me to tears for weeks afterwards. This was a decision that would come back to bite me in a couple of years, because I hadn't really processed the loss. Instead, I opted to throw myself into being busy for every waking minute. With the World's Strongest Disabled Man around the corner, I was glad I had such a big competition to take my mind off grieving.

I'd gone into "Britains" still built more like a bodybuilder, so I used these months to really live like a Strongman, with the help and support of Rob, a good friend and fellow Grenadier, who provided me with a place to train. My Strongman equipment took up a large part of the unit he used to take group training and PT sessions, but he was happy to help me set up and pack away, for which I was hugely grateful.

I increased my calories massively and, in terms of strength and energy, I could feel the benefits from early on. I altered my training to include Strongman-specific routines twice a week and would be in the gym three times a week. I added in pizzas, cheesecake, shakes consisting of full fat cream, ice cream, scoops of protein powder, scoops of peanut butter, honey and fruit three times a day – as well as my normal meals. My appearance was secondary, I didn't really have much concern for how I looked, just if my lifts were improving. A novice mistake on my part, still just really feeling my way into the sport, was to approach the

"Worlds" in the same way I approached bodybuilding. I trained right up until the day before the competition, wanting to give myself every possible chance of doing well. I knew I was going against the best in the world, and it played on my mind a lot.

This was, as I'd find out, a mistake – and one I'd never make again.

We·made our way up to Manchester the night before and I felt nervous – excited. I felt I'd invested a lot of effort in my training, and I'd certainly put on weight. I'd hardly slept and I woke up on the morning of the competition feeling lethargic – tired and aching. On speaking to the other lads I was competing alongside, most had had a minimum of four day's rest in the lead up to the competition, resting, recovering and taking on calories that their bodies could use on the day. I knew then that I'd messed up.

As we arrived at the Trafford Centre, we learned that the organisers had altered the events. Having a degree of OCD in my training, this threw me. I'd now be pulling the truck, a nine-tonne cab, sat in a wheelchair and with no place to press or rest my feet against. Consequently, it would be a much heavier pull than the one I'd done at "Britains" and a much harder technique. There was no mention of this in the weeks leading up to the day and frustration was an understatement. With the wheelchair slipping and turning from left to right and with the spotters told that they weren't to hold the chairs still, it was the worst possible start for me personally. My wheelchair twisted almost on the first pull and I was pulling the truck almost side on. My back was in agony and I sat a disheartening last place after event one, having moved the truck barely two metres.

As we moved onto event two, there were yet more changes for the log press. The bench had been moved into an upright position, as opposed to an incline. This meant it would be near on impossible for me to press, with the full weight emphasised solely on the deltoids, as opposed to some being transferred to the pectorals. I was first up, having finished joint last on the truck pull and the second I took full control of the log, it was pulling me forward. I couldn't arch my back enough, as I was strapped tight to the bench, to allow me to use my chest and triceps in the movement. After three or four attempts to press it, the red mist took over and I threw the log to the ground, unstrapped myself and walked off. The day was one better forgotten, and, at that point, I wanted the ground to swallow me up.

The people in the crowd must have seen me as a spoilt brat, throwing my toys out of the pram and storming off. I sat on my own, a lump in my throat, and felt way out of my depth. I thought I didn't deserve to be at this level, but the British lads that qualified with me picked me up and used stories of their own experiences to help me forget the previous two events and start the competition afresh.

The deadlift was next up – but this too had been changed from a conventional bar to a trap bar, which altered my grip and body positions entirely. But I was one of the last men standing in this event and, very slowly, I crept up the leader board. I was now just about doing myself justice.

The crucifix hold (holding dumbbells out to the side in a crucifix-like position) was next up, and this was the event I was dreading. With my shoulder, I fully expected to drop the weights as soon as the whistle went, especially with how the day was going so far. To my surprise, it was one of my best events. Fuelled by frustration, I channelled it all into putting myself through pain to get a good result and, again, chipped away at the points.

On to the dumbbell medley – five dumbbells, each going up in weight, to be pressed and locked out with one arm, in a wheelchair. Only a couple of us made it to the last dumbbell, a giant weight, and I finished a respectable second.

I now didn't want the competition to finish!

The final event was the atlas stones, but yet more changes to the equipment meant my wheelchair had a table fitted that was so wide, each atlas stone almost had to be thrown in order to get it onto the oil barrel on the other side. From the offset, this had been a poor competition in terms of changes and equipment, and it was a reality check for me.

I finished sixth overall and I was definitely happy with that, having been in last place after two events. Rather than being down for long and giving up, I chose to use it as a platform to get better. These lads were the best in the sport, so I picked the brains of the top five, and rest and recovery were the key things to take away from their advice. Greg, who I'd really built a good friendship with, booked the pair of us a trip to Swindon to train with none other than Laurence Shahlaei!

Having two hours of Laurence watching us train, correcting faults and giving us tips, was priceless. That man, single-handed, turned my log press from my weakest event into one of my best – all through turning my head to the side to allow me to rest the log on my chest more. Such a tiny adjustment made a world of difference, and I couldn't have been more grateful.

Wanting to put the disappointment of the "Worlds" to rest and finish the year strong, I entered Trojan Gym's Southwest of England's Strongest Disabled Man in Bristol. I wanted to put into practice all the advice Laurence had given us, and I felt great. I did no training for four days before the competition, which felt alien to me, but I had so much energy on the day. I was itching to get started, the complete opposite to how I woke up feeling in Manchester. Every event went great, even finishing second on the log press – Loz's technique made a huge difference. I finished that competition in second place, half a point behind the winner, Dave Walsh, another ex-squaddie. He'd competed in able-bodied Strongman before his MS took a hold of his everyday mobility. We had that same squaddie mentality and sense of humour, and I took to him instantly.

2017 saw Disabled Strongman included at the "infamous" Arnold Classic in Columbus, Ohio – a huge sports festival endorsed and attended by none other than Arnold Schwarzenegger and renowned for being the heaviest Strongman competition in the world. Being the first event of this kind at the festival, this would be invitation-only and comprised of British, American and Canadian disabled strongmen. Although the "Worlds" hadn't gone as I hoped, my win at "Britains" led to me receiving an invitation. March 2017, I'd be heading to the States to compete against some of the best in the world again, this time in front of crowds of thousands of people. After the advice I'd taken on board from Laurence Shahlaei and seeing the benefits when I competed in Bristol, I definitely believed I could finish in the top three.

I asked my dad if he'd like to come over with me, as Natalie was tied down with work and the boys were in school. It would be great to spend some time with him, and the other British lads heading over were great people too. So we all booked the same hotel in Columbus and had a few days before competing to adjust to the time difference – and the cold. March in Columbus was freezing! We met up for meals with the American lads, who were also brilliant, and the whole experience of that "Arnolds" was one of my best in Strongman – aside from sharing a room with my dad, who snored horrendously loud. I'm pretty sure he woke most mornings to find his bed covered in things I threw at him during the night.

It was electric walking around the convention centre, having time to watch the professionals up on stage in both Strongman and bodybuilding and seeing legends like Bill Kazmaier up close. Arnold Schwarzenegger could be spotted from afar, as an entourage of no less than twenty security guards in yellow shirts accompanied him everywhere. For us, the competition was close and highly contested, yet we all sat together, laughing in between events, almost as if the contest was a distraction from how well we all clicked. It relaxed us, and we all supported each other.

I won the sled pull and the atlas stones, both of which I'd worked on endlessly in the months following the "Worlds", and I found a good blend of aggression and technique in these two particular events. Everyone had strong points and these two were quickly becoming mine. I was now seeing that the experience of the "Worlds" was the best thing that could have happened to me. The recovery time before competing was helping, too. I'd be fidgeting before the first event, as I'd loaded up on good food in the days leading up to competing. I'd taken on board lots of advice on technique and had moved to a new house, quickly reserving the big garage for all my Strongman equipment!

Without going into too much detail, I won the Arnold Classic, and it was a dream come true. Arnold Schwarzenegger was an idol of mine from when I was a young boy. I knew all about the "Arnolds" – it was the World Cup of strength competitions, and to win it was overwhelming. People who trained in Atlas knew all about the magnitude of winning that particular competition – it meant I was one of the best in the world.

I was so immensely proud!

I'd been quietly adding more and more kit to the garage. I now had ropes, tyres, atlas stones, barrels, dumbbells and deadlifting bars. I bought equipment for every possible event and I had them set up exactly as they would be in competition, so that competing would feel like just another day in the garage. All my equipment was heavier than it would be in actual events, so that the real thing would seem a little bit easier than the training. Psychology! A couple of weeks before competing, I'd train the full repertoire in my garage, knowing I had the endurance and stamina to go flat out in every event. I reassured Natalie that this was an investment which would pay off and, sure enough, it did. 2017 was a great year, firstly winning the Arnold Classic in Ohio and then retaining my Britain's Strongest Disabled Man title two months later. I was getting heavier and heavier with each competition, which was starting to cause a bit of an issue with walking, but I was on such a high that it seemed a worthwhile sacrifice at the time.

I felt immensely proud to win "Britains" for the second time, as I wanted to prove that the first time wasn't a fluke. It was a competition that went down to the wire and the millisecond. A new athlete, Martin – also ex Forces – had entered, and when he arrived, he turned everyone's heads. He was huge, he looked the part before even touching a weight. There were more than a few murmurs that he would easily win, and this brought the best out in me and him. He won the deadlift and the Viking press, with me finishing second on both. I was still confident that I could do well in the remaining events and, although doubt crept in for those around me, I felt great and I loved that the two of us were fighting it out together. It was good for the sport and good for the atmosphere. We went one after the other, barely separated in our times or repetitions and, in truth, seeing the size of him, I was proud that I was giving him a battle. To look at, he was levels above me, but I knew I could put myself through hell to win that title again.

I won the sled pull and the dumbbell medley, with Martin's times a fraction slower. So, it all came down to the last event, my favourite – the atlas stones. He set a phenomenally fast time and I had to match it or better it to retain my title, it was that tight. I beat him by a second, if that. The relief, but also respect I had for Martin, was huge. It created an exciting rivalry and I knew Martin would come back stronger, which was exactly what I needed to keep me pushing.

We'd both qualified for the "Worlds", which would be at the Olympic Park in London that year. My time away from training was being spent public speaking, and it was great to get the chance to speak in the assembly at my sons' school. I loved the motivational side of what I was doing, and I was grateful that people had enough of an interest in it to ask me along to speak publicly. Keeping busy was suiting me and focusing on the "Worlds" was a chance to bury the previous experience.

A couple of days later, I found myself on a last-minute flight to Iceland. I always wanted to visit that country, the native home of

Strongman. Greg and Tony were flying out to compete in the Strongest Disabled Viking and the thought of a bit of a jolly was too good to turn down – supporting two top lads and getting to tick this place off the bucket list. On arriving in the Viking Village and seeing the set up, I was tempted to compete myself, but I was only there to support my friends. Hapfthor Julius Bjornsson made an appearance, and being stood with him made me feel like a little child in comparison.

Iceland was a surreal place, with twenty-four hours of daylight in the summer months, so we'd come out of a bar and it would still be bright. Following the competition, we were treated to some Icelandic delicacies – I really tried not to ask what they were – cold and slimy and on cocktail sticks. Not pleasant at all. They were an acquired taste to say the least, but their vodka, which was kept in a freezer, went down much easier.

Greg and Tony were great blokes to be around, and the social aspect of the sport was as appealing to me as the thrill of pulling trucks. I regularly met with Dan, Greg and Tony to train and it was those times that I valued more than any trophies. With us all qualifying for the "Worlds", we had a real motivation to push us and, with different strong points, we could all help each other to improve. Strongman is largely dependant on what events are involved at a particular competition and I was fortunate with "Britains" that all five events were ones I liked. But, as the events were announced for the "Worlds", the front hold stood out for me – holding a Thor's Hammer out to the front for as long as possible.

I knew straight away it would be difficult to win the competition – looking at the names of those who'd qualified, I'd be likely to come last in the front hold event, which would cost me a lot of points. With it being the "Worlds", the weights naturally increase from national level and the Thor's Hammer would weigh 22.5kg. I practiced and practiced in my garage, but even a 15kg hammer was proving difficult. I knew I needed to mentally write this event off and, rather than approaching the competition on a low, focus on the other events, which I knew I could do well in.

The opening event was a van pull, on a slight incline and with the van full of weight. I'd been working on getting myself fired up, rather than enjoying a laugh until it was my turn. It had to be more serious this time, and I went off for five minutes, taking in big inhalations of smelling salts and really working myself up into an almost frenzied state. It couldn't have worked better for the van pull and I was so focused on only looking at the rope that I continued pulling even when the van was over the finish line. I wiped out the memory of the awful truck pull I had at the previous "Worlds" and that's what fired me up – failure. I found it hard to calm down afterwards; my emotions were still high and the adrenaline was well and truly flowing. After a few minutes' reflection, I went over to Natalie to enjoy the moment of winning the first event. I took the attitude that if it wasn't broken, don't try to fix it – and so the "Worlds" continued throughout the day like that.

I did well in the Viking press and finished, as expected, in last place on the Thor's Hammer. From the moment the whistle went, I was struggling to hold it out straight, but I didn't let it get to me. It was the next event that would frustrate me more – the sandbag loading race. Four sandbags, increasing in size and weight, to be placed on our laps and wheeled to the opposite side, some twenty metres away. My first three flew, but the wheelchair, the same one for each of us, was causing me problems. It wasn't cut out for these weights and was far from robust enough. The wheel locked up and the tyre came off and I was stuck. No second chances – that was my go finished. It left a bitter taste, as others seemed to get second goes in events where kit and equipment broke.

I knew the hammer would be my nemesis, but I thought I'd do well on the loading race – yet a broken wheelchair had cost me. Even once it was repaired, there was no second go, and, despite going on to finish with a win on the atlas stones – the only person on the day to win two events – I finished a disappointing fourth. The consolation was that Greg won the "Worlds" and, putting my own frustration to one side, I was really pleased for him. He'd been consistent throughout and deserved to hold his head high as the best in the world.

But new faces in Strongman (I won't name names) were bringing an entourage with them to every competition and disputing every decision. The sport began to lose the togetherness that made it so special and had made the first "Arnolds" the enjoyable experience it was. Being at the very top of the sport, I was seen as direct competition. I had more than a few run-ins with guys like this, and I had buttons that these people knew how to press.

I was gradually becoming driven by the prospect of beating them rather than enjoying myself, and I could feel that I was reacting when I knew it was the wrong thing to do. They had no interest in knowing me as a person and saw me only as someone who needed to be beaten. Little did they know, in the months following the "Worlds", my walking was nearly non-existent. I had an exploratory operation on my sciatic nerve which, had it worked, would have eased the pains I was experiencing in the back of my leg and helped with the flexion of my hip. Sadly, it didn't work and made my walking and pain levels worse than ever.

I was finding myself heading out to the garage with the intention to train, only to sit there in silence. Day by day, I was losing any enthusiasm – I was driven purely by anger. This came to a head when a Disabled Strongman competition was organised in Milton Keynes: Milton Keynes' Strongest Disabled Man. It was my hometown and I was the only athlete in the sport that was from Milton Keynes, and I didn't even get invited to compete. It was organised by someone who was, how should I say, not very fond of me, and it felt like a kick in the teeth. I reacted badly, which was what was wanted, I think.

Despite silently struggling by this point, I was able to put on a happy face in front of all who weren't in our family home, and I was humbled that my efforts in the sport were deemed worthy enough for people to put me forward for a sporting excellence award in the Soldiering On awards – a prestigious awards evening, held in Westminster, alongside men and women who'd completed amazing feats, both as serving soldiers and as injured veterans. I listened to their stories and felt that my achievements were minimal compared to some, which included rowing the Atlantic! I didn't win the category, but I felt so privileged to even be in the same room as some genuinely awe-inspiring individuals.

Following that, I'd be off to the "Arnolds" again in March 2018. My focus wasn't on retaining that title because it would fill me with pride, it was on having the last laugh. I became obsessive, in an unhealthy way. I was being driven from a sport because I was competition. You see, I was doing well and, through no canvassing of my own, I was being offered exciting opportunities on television, and resentment and jealousy had grown towards me. I was left feeling more and more like an outsider in a sport that had become toxic for me.

This, in addition to the increasing pain, plus still not really talking much about Spence and missing the army more and more, landed me in a bad place. It was fuelled, without doubt, by the fact I was feeling alone and spiralling into depression. I was trying to keep a lid on it at home, Strongman was something I could channel my feelings into, but I no longer enjoyed the sport. I flew to the "Arnolds", after a three-hour delay at Heathrow, missing my connecting flight in New York and then having to fly to Charlotte and then on to Columbus. I arrived late at night and lost my baggage, and neither my dad nor the lads who had competed the year before were with me this time. It was a very different experience.

These new faces and their entourages had well and truly killed off that togetherness of us all meeting for meals and supporting each other. Instead, at the athletes briefing, I was greeted with cold shoulders and silence, but the competition had five events that were great for me. I was at my heaviest, 120kg, but in agony. I could barely walk and was sweating after a minute of trying. The walking made the pain in my sciatic nerve worse, and the pain made my mood worse. I was just thankful that the American lads were as welcoming and accommodating as the year before.

This year, the competition was held over two days and the first day was the dumbbell medley. I was one of only two to press the 65kg dumbbell; a third competitor pressed it after the whistle, which was only disputed with the referee the following day.

There was no socialising, and that evening ended with me sat back in my room, happy I was currently in first, but disappointed with the different atmosphere this time around. I woke up for the second day determined to stay in front, but another wheelchair malfunction on yet another loading race meant the second day got off to a dreadful start. I went on to win the remaining events – the sled pull, the atlas stones and the kettlebell hold. I was sat in first going into the final event, when suddenly the dumbbell medley from the day before became an issue. The referee on the second day wasn't the same guy and he was swayed into changing the points, and I was, somehow, despite winning all but one event, going into the kettlebell hold in second!

This just ignited my absolute determination to win, no matter how much pain the last event might put me in. I wasn't going to lose now. John, an American who was also angry at the late change to the points, which caused him to drop down a place, offered to call out the time for me in the hold. I held on and held on and won, and I think John cheered more than me. I'd always been respectful enough to never celebrate out loud, but this time I was ecstatic. I received my trophy to silence, and within half an hour, I was sat back in my hotel room.

It was a surreal, yet sad experience.

I went on to win England's Strongest Disabled Man a few weeks later at Brands Hatch racetrack and then finish second at Britain's Strongest Disabled Man in May. The atmosphere backstage at "Britains" in the athletes' briefing, where the rules were discussed, was a bit toxic. I asked if I could bring up why I was being singled out and why so much negativity was being fired my way recently in relation to sponsors and stuff. Nobody cared to comment when it was put straight to their faces – they preferred to talk behind my back..

Inside, I was falling apart and, although my name was down to compete at the "Worlds" in Norway, I wasn't looking forward to it. I was hoping our family holiday to Florida beforehand would be the pick-me-up I needed.

How wrong I was.

Grenadier Day: Showing the Boys the 50 cal heavy machine gun, in Lille Barracks, Aldershot

Spence's resting place

Ellis wrote this letter at school to cheer me up after he had seen me crying the morning I found out Spence had passed away

Training day with Laurence Shahlaei, 2016: Quite possibly the most insightful two hours I had in Strongman. Loz helped to improve my technique in just about every event

Arnold Classic, Columbus, Ohio, 2017: Being congratulated on winning the Arnolds by Brian Shaw. I felt like a ten-year-old boy stood with his dad!

Arnold Classic 2017: With Dan Piggott, Magnus ver Magnusson and one of the nicest men I have ever had the pleasure of meeting, Darren Stanesby

Britain's Strongest Disabled Man 2017: Sat proudly with my two boys and the Britain's Strongest Disabled Man trophy

Surrounded by amazing men and women of our Armed Forces, who had all been nominated for a Soldiering On award

Soldiering On awards night: Stood proudly with my wife at the awards night in London

Eddie Hall: Sat with the World's Strongest Man and first man to deadlift 500kg, a genuine idol of mine in the sport

Britain's Strongest Disabled Man 2018: The pull. Whether it was a truck, van, car or sled, I loved this event. An event that requires focus and aggression in equal measure

Britain's Strongest Disabled Man 2018: My favourite event, the atlas stones. Winning the event by 12 seconds and finishing on a high

14

ROCK BOTTOM

Training for the "Worlds" in Norway felt like a chore and I was really struggling to motivate myself. The pain in my leg was making concentration on anything difficult – it was a no-win situation. I knew my weight was helping in competitions and I was feeling the strongest and most consistent all round that I'd felt since venturing into Strongman. But it was my weight that was undoubtedly contributing to the level of pain I was in. My mind was telling me the sensible thing to do would be to lose weight so I could walk better but, with the level of athletes consistently rising, I knew losing weight would see me fall behind. I didn't want to be in the middle of the pack, but I was equally worried about what I'd do if I gave up Strongman and didn't have anything to challenge me.

I was still concerned with filling the void that the army had left and I was using sport to fill that void, which seemed to overrule the importance of my health. By now, it wasn't just my leg that was struggling to cope, but my overall health was being affected by the parts of Strongman not really seen. Natalie often had to nudge me in the night, as sleeping on my back affected my breathing and I was experiencing sleep apnoea. My wife was beginning to question if competing three times a year was worth the suffering for the other 362 days.

A welcome distraction was the 2018 FIFA World Cup in Russia and, with England doing so well, a boyhood dream came to life. My mates thought it was a heat of the moment decision, but I was deadly serious. Despite being barely able to walk, following England's win over Sweden, I was on a flight to Moscow forty-eight hours later. As far back as Italia 90, I dreamt of following England at a World Cup and, even though we were due to go on our family holiday to Florida in a couple of weeks, I convinced Natalie that it would be fine and I'd be back with time to spare. I think she was glad that my mind would be taken away from Strongman while I was there.

The flight over from Heathrow was full of England fans, and the atmosphere on the plane for the entirety of the trip was electrifying – singing and drinking, much like the flight over to Jamaica, minus the Company Sergeant Major to tear us off a strip later. We made our way to the hotel on landing and I'd picked a place with a big Russian powerlifting gym next door. I was going to enjoy the whole experience, but I was also conscious that I still needed to train. The gym was brilliant – everyone seemed to look like Wladimir Klitschko and no one spoke English, but it was perfect. The food, however, was questionable. Our hotel wasn't exactly in the tourist part of Moscow, so it was all Russian cuisine for breakfast, which was an anti-climax after training. I mean, "full English" it certainly wasn't – more a mixture of peas, cucumber and fish. Not really to my taste first thing in the morning, and I lived off boiled eggs for the week!

After training and eating, we jumped in a taxi and headed into Red Square to join the thousands of England fans congregating and celebrating. It was a carnival atmosphere, just how I'd dreamt a World Cup would be. People playing football in front of the Kremlin, an English bar heaving and plenty of singing, as well as long queues for the only decent place to eat in Red Square – KFC! Moscow wasn't great for making things accessible and I didn't see many people, be it locals or football fans, with disabilities. There was a lot of walking, which was getting worse for me but, funnily enough, I was finding the beer was helping to numb the pain.

I knew that would be a slippery slope to go down.

The day of the semi-final against Croatia was spent sat outside the hotel bar waiting for a courier to deliver our match tickets. The minute they arrived, we jumped into a taxi to the Luzhniki Stadium and made our way through the turnstiles. I'm pretty sure that moment was the most I'd ever grinned – aside from my wedding day and birth of my boys! On finding our seats were seven rows behind the goal and looking round to see a sea of England flags, I got a lump in my throat and my eyes filled with tears. I was at a World Cup semi-final, with England potentially ninety minutes from the final, and I was here! After all those years of watching on television and being just as drawn in by the atmosphere of the England fans as I was with the game, this was absolutely top of my bucket list. I phoned Natalie and I'm pretty sure I spent the first minute of the call just thanking her for making it a reality.

By the time the game kicked off, I'd almost lost my voice and, within four minutes, I nearly lost my leg as well. A Kieran Trippier free kick put us 1-0 up and I fell back into the row behind with fully grown men in tears of joy, kissing each other and jumping hysterically. I've never taken recreational drugs, but I'm pretty sure that the initial high isn't a patch on how I felt at that moment. The lads in front of us were brilliant and one had returned from the bar with drinks for us all, just as Trippier stepped up to take the free kick. As I fell back, my prosthetic leg stayed in the row in front of my seat and now I was wearing eight freshly-poured beers! I'm positive that not one of us had even taken a sip!

As history will tell, we went on to lose the game in extra time, and the tears of joy turned to sobbing. The following day, feeling deflated and realising the dream of seeing us play in a World Cup final was gone, we did some tourist stuff. Moscow's open-top bus route wasn't the most interesting, so we used it as a method of keeping an eye out for different pubs. Sitting outside a bar enjoying a beer and reflecting on the emotions of the game the night before, we made plans to fly to St. Petersburg to watch England play Belgium in the third-place game.

By contrast, St. Petersburg was full of colour, a beautiful place – aside from the fact that the stadium was a three-mile walk from the underground and surrounded by parks, meaning there was no way of getting a taxi. The walk was the straw that broke the camel's back – I was a sweaty, angry mess. I would go as far as to say that, out of the sixty thousand fans that left that stadium at the end of the game, we were the very last to get to the underground. I began to feel guilty, knowing that this one walk was going to really take its toll on me and that it would impact our holiday in Florida, which was now just a few days away.

Our week in Russia came to an end, and it was one I'll never forget. I'd ticked off a dream, although the results weren't quite what I'd wished for. The journey home, however, was far from a dream. It was a bad sign when our taxi to the airport came within inches of ploughing into the back of a petrol tanker because our driver fell asleep!

Our first flight took us to Lisbon in Portugal, where we wouldn't have long to catch our connecting flight. I could barely move and was on crutches, while wearing my prosthetic leg – slow was an understatement. The security as we came into customs in Lisbon asked me to put my crutches through the scanner, which is when things turned very sour. The scanners picked up on something in my crutches. Not thinking anything of it, I was more concerned that we were now going to miss our connecting flight. We did, but I was also now being taken away by armed police to a police station in Lisbon. A powder-like substance could be seen on the screen inside the poles of my crutches. I'd left them in our hotel when we flew from Moscow to St. Petersburg, and what initially seemed like a mix-up now had me worried as to whether anyone had tampered with them.

On getting out of the police car, I was led into a room with a team of narcotics officers, and at that point, my arse fell out a bit. I was asked questions about where we'd been and why and if anyone had used my crutches. We waited for an allen key, of all things, for the police to unscrew my crutches and empty out whatever these contents were. As the handles came off, a torch was shone into the hollow poles and they were smelled and passed around. Meanwhile, I had visions of being someone's girlfriend in a Portuguese prison.

The powder was poured out onto the table and it turned out to be mud! I'd taken part in an obstacle assault course years before, which involved a few river crossings. The feet of the crutches had both broken off in the water and, rather than stopping, I'd continued on the course, as it was to raise money for Blesma, the limbless veterans' charity. Once my crutches dried the next day, I'd simply replaced the feet and completely forgotten that the mud that had gotten inside would still be in them, and I'd taken them on holiday numerous times after that without any issues at any airports.

I was a relieved man. To say they looked disappointed that it wasn't drugs would not be an exaggeration. But they said I could go, and I was taken back to the airport. I now had to get a new connecting flight and find my mates. Our bags were nowhere to be seen, but the airline staff assured us they'd be at Luton Airport when we landed – they weren't. So, after our near-death collision on the Russian motorway, followed by the thought of being gang-banged in prison, I was now at Luton and my bags were missing – and I was flying to Florida in two days for our family holiday.

To make matters worse, on collecting my car at the airport, a tyre had been slashed. That euphoria of Trippier's goal was a distant, blurry memory now. I was hoping I was on some prank programme and Jeremy Beadle or someone would jump out to surprise me at any moment. But sadly not. One consolation: my bags were found in Lisbon and they were with me in time for our holiday. I was the envy of so many friends, having been to a World Cup, but I was suffering for it now, especially that one walk back from the stadium in St. Petersburg. I spent the day before our holiday, reluctantly, on my crutches. At that time, having not been around the people I'm around today in amputee football and realising that crutches were much more comfortable and easy to get around on, I was still in that Headley Court mindset of insisting I go on holiday on my prosthetic leg. From Natalie's face, I could see she was already dreading it.

Upon getting to Gatwick, I received messages that my name was dirt in Strongman, and they weren't well received. In the opinion of the friends I did make in the sport, it was all out of jealousy that I was getting the sponsors and magazine interviews and the like, as I'd concluded myself. In all honesty, most of those people were just interested in the fact that I'd been shot in Canada, of all places, and the sport was secondary to them. The interviews weren't things I desired, but I thought they'd help in growing the sport.

I was also frustrated that I could barely walk. My amputation and the exit wound from the bullets to my groin mean that, in hot weather, I sweated a lot and my prosthetic rubbed on the scar tissue, so the skin in my groin was worn down to raw red flesh. That walk back from the stadium had really left a mark on me, and it was only going to get worse.

After Russia, I made the bad decision not to take my crutches to Florida, as friends who'd been before said the hotels supplied wheelchairs. I wasn't best pleased about using a wheelchair in the first place and was dismayed to see the hotel staff in Florida push out this bloody monstrosity of a thing. It was wide enough to fit me and my boys sat next to each other on the seat. My heart sank a little, as it was too wide for me to wheel myself, so if I was going to use it, I'd be reliant on Natalie to push me. Natalie was apprehensive too, as she knew it was going to be a fight to get me into it when I needed a rest.

On the first day, admittedly sulking a bit, we made our way to Magic

Kingdom in Disney World. I insisted on pushing the wheelchair to the bus stop and folded it up so I could sit on a normal seat on the bus. The drivers were fantastic in how much they helped people with disabilities on and off, I certainly couldn't fault them at all, but I was just too proud and stubborn to admit I needed help. I felt I was too able bodied to be parked and clipped into the special harnesses for the wheelchairs, and I didn't want the folding chairs to have to be sacrificed for me, as that would mean fewer people could sit down. I stuck to my guns that first day and reluctantly got in the chair at points around the park only when it was clear I was slowing our family down and holding my sons back from seeing the characters and the rides they wanted to go on. It wasn't feeling like a dream holiday, but I was trying to smile whenever the boys looked in my direction.

In that first week, the time difference, humidity, wheelchair and the pain was making me horrible to be around. This reached a boiling point when we were off to one of the water parks and I didn't have my leg on, so I had to be wheeled onto the bus and harnessed in safely in full view of all the passengers. I wanted the ground to swallow me up – I felt humiliated, degraded and useless. Natalie tried to make light of it, but I was dying inside. All that dignity and pride I'd stubbornly been trying to hold onto was gone. At the park, I couldn't go on many of the slides, so I was left in different spots in my wheelchair while the family went off. I didn't want them missing out, but I was resenting my amputation massively at that moment. When the family came back, they said there was a slide I could go on as it had a chair lift up to it. The boys were so excited that that Daddy could go on with them.

My wheelchair had to be left with the staff at the bottom of the chair lift and I had to get into a water wheelchair, one with tiny wheels that went in all different directions at the same time and I had no control over. We got to the top, checked and double checked that I'd be able to ride before queuing, and was told I could. We got to the front and the lifeguard had changed, and this one said I couldn't go down – after the rest of my family had already slid off. I was now stuck at the top of this massive hill, with only steps down, in a wheelchair I couldn't manoeuvre on my own. My family had no idea I was left at the top, unable to get down, and for forty-five minutes, I sat there, utterly useless. I tried to hop down, using the wheelchair as a frame to support me, but the steps were wet and the wheelchair kept tipping back under my overweight frame.

So I sat waiting in the sun, feeling like the people queuing were staring relentlessly at me. Natalie came and got me when she realised, but I was emotionally done at that point. We had some food and went back to the hotel. On getting into the room, Natalie closed our door to ask if I was okay and I broke down. There had been highs since Spence died, there had been enjoyable family time and there was going to Russia. But I'd been putting on a false sense of being alright, to keep others happy. In my mind, I didn't want to be here anymore – I was tired of the constant pain, it was taking over my life. I couldn't think or concentrate without being distracted by my leg. I was missing the army, where I'd been one of the blokes. I was missing the lifestyle of being a soldier. I was being pushed out in Strongman just as I'd been pushed out in secondary school. I missed Spence. I wanted the pain in my leg and the pain inside my soul to go, and I could see it broke Natalie's heart when I told her I didn't want to live like this.

I'd tried various sockets for the discomfort in my leg, each one just as painful as the one before. I'd tried an operation on my sciatic nerve and a nerve block, which was excruciating – but nothing seemed to touch the pain. With Strongman turning toxic, I'd lost that sense of belonging, something that I'd been searching for since my medical discharge. I was anxious about the reception I'd receive if I went to compete at the "Worlds" in Norway – it upset me more than I let on. I always prided myself on being loyal and helping others, which I'd done time and time again in Strongman – putting others before myself, hosting fundraisers, opening up interviews that should have been for me to include everyone in the sport. I made programmes and radio shows open invitations to the other athletes to help them and to enable me to fit in, yet I was being ushered out. It was school all over again.

As much as I'd started to open up to Natalie about my current problems, I'd still never told her about school. I was embarrassed and ashamed and buried it, but it had undoubtedly played a part in how defensive and stubborn I'd become. The news about my dad not actually being my real dad and my mother's absolute refusal to tell me who my biological father was eating away at me, too. She promised to take it to her grave because she didn't want her past dug up when she wasn't even with that person anymore – and she was the only one who knew his name. I'm not sure that she ever once realised, that stuck in the middle of what turned out to be an affair, was me and the questions I had – did I have other siblings, would they want to know me, would they want to know my children?

I'd often cry when sat in the garage, unable to train, just sitting in a sorry state talking to Spence – which probably seems a little odd to those reading this. Whenever I was driving on my own, I'd envisage crashing my car into the wall on the stretch of motorway between Luton and Milton Keynes. Then I'd be overcome with guilt for even beginning to think like that. I felt selfish that I could let those thoughts enter my head when I was a dad and a husband.

It was like my mind never switched off, and the dam broke in that hotel room in Florida. I finally admitted to Natalie that I believed I was depressed and needed help. Having been a proud Grenadier Guard, a leader, a practical joker, a winner in Strongman and bodybuilding, the humiliation I felt on the bus and the water park that day was the lowest I'd ever been. But hopefully, through realising that I needed help, I'd hit rock bottom and the only way was back up. At that point, opening up even a small amount to Natalie felt like a big weight had been lifted from my shoulders, and I phoned my casualty officer from the Grenadiers, while sat in our hotel room, to ask if I could see a counsellor. I said I'd withdraw from the World's Strongest Disabled Man competition, to remove that added burden, and promised to let Natalie look after me by pushing me in the wheelchair, as she wanted to do. The rest of the holiday was an improvement, and I was determined to be smiling when it was Ethan's birthday – we'd booked for us to swim with dolphins at Discovery Cove.

When we got home, it was time to face the reality of all I said I'd do once we were back. Wanting to be proactive, we sat together and wrote a list. It included all the positive things in life and all the negatives, and how we could change the negatives. I said I missed the army, that sense of humour and belonging. I said I'd love to play football again and to be back in a team. As much as Strongman and bodybuilding had been a success, spending so much time in my own company wasn't healthy. I said I wanted to look at going into private care to find a suitable, comfortable socket. I said I wanted to lose weight.

As if by fate, not long after, I received an invititation to be considered to appear on the television programme Dr Christian's Special Clinics. I phoned the next day to say that message had come at the perfect time, as I was really struggling with the sciatic nerve in my leg.

It was now time to accept any help that was willingly being sent my way and to sort myself out. I needed to put into practise those positives and the things I wanted to do again and prove I was serious about getting help.

I knew if I didn't, it could have a big impact on my marriage.

FIFA World Cup 2018: Stood outside the Luzhniki Stadium in Moscow, Russia, before England v Croatia, ticking off a boyhood dream

Orlando, Florida, 2018: Sat with my stepdaughter, Lucy, and my two boys, Ellis and Ethan

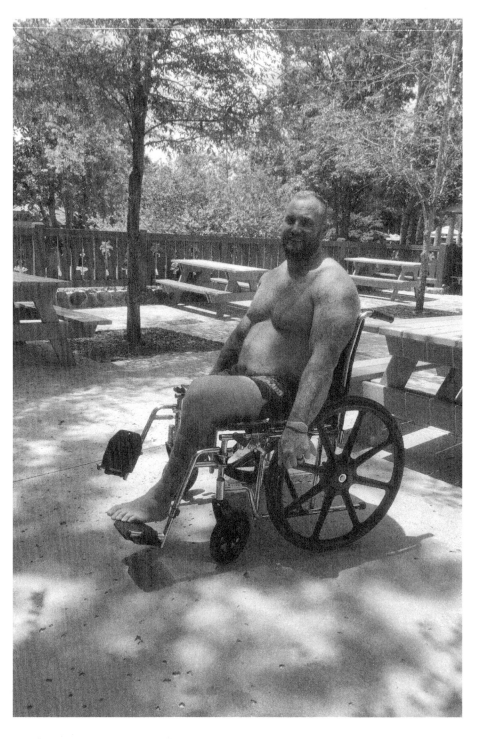

Blizzard Beach, Orlando, Florida, 2018: The day that I broke down and realised I needed help

15

NEW BEGINNINGS

September 2018 should have seen me competing in Norway at what would have been my third World's Strongest Disabled Man. Although I wasn't happy in the sport, I still felt that it was a year where I could have improved on the fourth place I'd ended up in the previous year. Instead, I was scrolling through counsellors in the area who specialised in post-traumatic stress, depression and suicide. The Grenadier Guards agreed to fund counselling sessions for as long as I felt I needed them and I found one close by – a little old lady called Pat who ran her sessions from the conservatory at her home. I booked in, but I was hesitant and kept my barriers up. The first appointment consisted of filling out questionnaires on whether I had thoughts of committing suicide. That was my first obstacle: swallowing my pride and not just ticking "no", but admitting that those very thoughts had run through my head daily.

I tried to start each day afresh, telling myself it would be better. Then I'd look at my prosthetic leg propped up against the wall next to the bed, and the dread would build up. I'd delay getting out of bed for as long as I could, as I knew that was the last point in the day when I'd be relatively pain free. I'd fit the leg on and, with that very first step, weight bear through the stump would almost make me whimper at the pain. Unlike discomforts I'd had in the past, this pain wouldn't ease off, but just get progressively worse as the day went on. It was dictating my social life, as I'd turn down the chance to see friends because I knew that would involve walking and, at that time in my life, there was no way I was going out of the house if I wasn't on my prosthetic leg. Natalie didn't understand this, but Headley Court's crack-on mentality was well and truly engrained in me. But it was also ruining me.

My mood was dictated by the level of pain, so I was horrible to be around – snappy, irritable and unable to think clearly without this pain overruling what I was doing. I was losing enjoyment in everything and had become something of a shell. With each unsuccessful appointment at the limb fitting centre, I'd drive home disheartened and feeling worse than before I'd gone there. I'd still get my hopes up that each appointment would be the turning point, but with every adjustment unable to help, I was having more and more suicidal thoughts and the enormous guilt that came with them. The reality was, I wanted to live, but I also needed help and, up to now, didn't have the backbone to ask for it. I just saw myself as a burden to my family. I'd lost any zest for life – so, in answer to whether I had suicidal thoughts, I answered "yes" on the questionnaire.

Over the next six weeks or so, I visited Pat for an hour at a time and we talked about everything from birth to breaking point., which is largely why I felt I should put my childhood into words in this book. Once she linked my personality and my thought process to my experiences growing up, a lot began to fit together and make sense. At first, I wondered why schooldays had any relevance to dealing with how Spence died and the depression I'd sunk into. The turning point came on the day Pat spent the entire hour asking me to recall what school was like. Again I was hesitant and just wanted to say it was fine, but I thought there must have been a reason why she was asking. So I opened up. Within minutes, I found myself crying in front of this counsellor and crying on the way home, too. I'd buried those feelings deep inside and, fuelled by the need to prove myself strong, had been in denial ever since.

Natalie always asked me how each appointment went, and sometimes I'd leave it a couple of days before I told her, just to digest all that had come up. After this appointment, I felt compelled to ask her if we could have a talk. The way I sat her down and how nervous I looked, she must have thought I had really bad news, but I got it all off my chest. I related the severity of the bullying, and it felt like a big, dark cloud had disappeared. I'd kept this quiet from Natalie for thirteen years – we knew almost everything about each other, but I'd always kept this stored at the back of my mind, convinced she'd think less of me as a man. In her own words, she was disappointed that I hadn't felt I could talk to her sooner, but she now understood a lot of my behaviour and said parts of my personality made more sense.

One part she highlighted was that, in pub fights back when I was in the army, I could never just walk away – I had to stick up for my friends, regardless of the outcome. It was for two reasons: firstly, I was so grateful to finally have genuine friends, and secondly, I knew what it felt like to have people run off and leave me on my own and I could never do that to anyone else. I remembered being attacked in the shopping centre back when I was young – five youths approached me and I was hit with a knuckle duster, breaking my nose and covering the floor with blood as I fell to the ground. As I looked up, people just left me there to fend for myself. Eventually, I was taken to hospital where my nose was repaired, and I had to give a statement to the police – but no charges were ever brought.

When you think about it, it was child abuse of the worst kind. Again, I don't want to name names, but if any of those people are reading this, they'll know who they are. Child abuse is a crime, no matter how long ago it happened. I hope they realise that and will feel some semblance of shame for the cowardly way they behaved back then – because all bullying is the realm of cowards. It's the bully who's the lesser person, the skulker in the shadows, not the bullied. It took me a long time to realise that.

Once I'd told Natalie all of it, she finally began to see the real me, who I was deep inside, and she started to understand why I behaved the way I did. I also began to accept myself at last. Opening up to her like that was the first time I felt truly at ease and, at that point, I realised the benefits I could get from counselling.

As the weeks went on, Pat couldn't shut me up, and together we built a picture of how my brain had been wired from disappointment, grief and feeling alone – many of the feelings I'd recently begun to relive in Strongman. My brain was reverting to the mindset of my teenage self. Pat asked me what I'd say to my teenage self if he was sat next to me at that moment.

"Stand up for yourself! Fight back!"

That was my initial response, but when I thought a bit more about it, a more mature response was probably:

"Respect yourself. Don't allow them to destroy your self-esteem."

We got onto the subject of the revelation that my dad wasn't my biological father and how that had eaten away at me. I knew my mother was never going to tell me who my biological father was, but Pat asked if I really wanted to know, and if I did, what was stopping me? So I picked away at that scab and started, once again, to see if I could find out where I really came from. I wondered if I had siblings I knew nothing about – maybe even uncles, aunts, cousins – and I wondered, if they found out I existed, would they treat me better than my own family?

A lot of pent-up resentment and hatred was coming out – and I don't use those words lightly. I never bought into the saying "you only have one mum", and it was hatred I felt towards my mother. She seemed to want to cause me nothing but pain, and her utter selfishness had been demonstrated during my time at Headley Court. I discovered in 2012, with the Grenadiers away on Op Herrick 16, that the lad she'd been seeing while I was in Afghanistan had been shot in the head and wasn't in a good way. One of the lads pointed him out to me on the neurological wing and he was unrecognisable – apparently missing part of his head, and clearly suffering from life changing injuries. Any feelings of negativity I'd had towards him were gone in an instant. I just felt sorry for him; he was still a Grenadier and I knew how manipulative my mother could be. I always tried to pride myself on not being like her in any way. That's a large part of why I grew a beard and had my neck tattooed, so I couldn't see her when I looked in the mirror.

I phoned Natalie that evening to tell her what I'd found out, and she said that telling my mother seemed like the right thing to do. Natalie offered to do it, but my mother's response put the nail in the coffin of any relationship I might have had with her.

"Why would I care?"

I was disgusted. This was exactly her attitude towards me wanting to find my biological father – it all had to be about her. She had no concept of anyone else's feelings.

Concurrent to attending my counselling sessions, I'd been given funding by the Grenadiers to try a private prosthetic socket for my leg. I researched the comfort aspect and the different techniques used and, on visiting a small family business called Poldark Prosthetics in Watford, run by a group of Italians, I was excited to finally find what I hoped would be a comfortable socket. The ability to walk comfortably would be life changing at this point. It seemed that one piece of good news followed another, as I was invited down to London as one of the patients who'd be seen on the Dr Christian programme. With the prospect of Harley Street open to me, I was growing increasingly more optimistic that Florida would be as low as I would get.

Away from my appointments with Pat, I started to tick off some of the things I'd written on my list of solutions to my problems. I began attending a walking football session once a week. It's a sport that doesn't get the credit it deserves, allowing people over fifty to get on a football pitch and to socialise. I saw it as an ideal environment to get used to playing on crutches, to try to lose some of the Strongman weight and to be around people again. I was welcomed from the moment I turned up to my first session, despite being the only amputee, and once my confidence on the crutches started to grow, I began to love being on a pitch again. At that point, I had no plans to play competitively and was aware that I was way below the level required to play amputee football. But it was nice to have something to look forward to each week and not have any pressure on myself. For the first time in years I was doing something where I could just enjoy the moment.

I began to spend more time on crutches, realising I didn't have to be on my prosthetic leg all the time and I could get about a bit quicker. I could wake up and not dread putting my leg on. It was nice to wake up and feel like the day had got off to a positive start, although I still wanted a comfortable prosthetic given the choice. As the weeks went on, I settled into the walking football and found that there were more sessions like it elsewhere, so I started to attend those too, and, inevitably, that itch to take things further began to resurface.

Back in my counselling appointments, it was good to start the hour off by telling Pat positive things, and now that I'd opened up more to Natalie at home, being open with Pat no longer worried me. I bought into her methods and felt comfortable with all but one, EMDR (Eye Movement Desensitization and Reprocessing) – reliving traumatic experiences while following some moving red lights from left to right. I just didn't get it, and although I tried to give it time, the more I was asked how it was making me feel, the more I was getting irritated. To Pat's credit, she acknowledged this and told wasn't something I had to stick with. I felt more comfortable having a conversation with someone who had an unbiased view, with different methods for processing these moments. Then the subject came up that, although I knew it was coming, I still dreaded – talking about Spence and the hole his passing had left. I can say quite openly that I cried for just about the entirety of that hour-long appointment. But, week by week, I was feeling happier and I could honestly write in the weekly question sheet that I had no thoughts of not wanting to be here.

Then came my leg fitting – the private socket was ready. The best way I can think to describe the old socket is that it was like wearing a stiletto full of stinging nettles that had a clamp either side, screwed up tight and set on fire! I couldn't wait for them to remove it, and, within a few steps, the new socket took the pressure away from my sciatic nerve, the exit wound scarring in my groin and a painful area of heterotopic ossification (a claw-shaped bone that grows on the femur and is common in amputees) on the outside of my stump. I went from a painful stiletto to a soft slipper! My smile would have made the Cheshire Cat from Alice in Wonderland look miserable by comparison.

I drove home grinning all the way, passing the very bridge I'd envisaged crashing into just months earlier. I felt relaxed in my seat, without fidgeting, and was able to concentrate on driving, not distracted by pain. I couldn't wait to get home and walk and pick my boys up for a cuddle. It had been a while since I'd been able to do that.

As the days went on, I was able to put my leg on first thing in the morning and just walk, and I could get up from a chair without bracing myself for the pain of that first step. It was literally life changing, and I now wanted to be out socialising – I wanted to go out as a family for the day. Although this was a huge improvement, I still had the Dr Christian programme to help further.

The day of filming came along and, on arriving at the hospital, we were taken to the green room for the patients who'd be appearing on the programme. The producers had already been given my backstory and the pain that I wanted help with. Natalie was called in for her interview in front of the cameras, and then it was my turn. It was only once it had been aired on television that I really took on board just how much this had affected Natalie too, yet she'd been by my side throughout. I told myself that hopefully, after this television opportunity, I could make it up to her. It was the first time I told anyone, aside from Natalie, Pat and my casualty officer, just how low I'd got, so to be open in front of the cameras and admit that I'd wanted to end my life earlier in the year was a big moment.

Our turn to go in and see the doctor was all a bit surreal, as it was a top floor at a hospital in London that had cameras everywhere. We had microphones attached to us all day, so I had to hold in a fart that really needed letting go! The waiting area and the doors into the surgery were all part of the stage set-up and it felt a bit odd walking through four or five times so they could film it from different angles. The lady on the desk was answering a pretend phone, which amused me highly, while we sat in the waiting room. After going in to see Dr Sara Kayat, botox injections were suggested to treat the pain in my sciatic nerve, and I was more than willing to try.

I made my way next door to the doctor who'd be carrying out the injections, when I suddenly remembered how horrific the nerve block I'd had done previously was. That particular needle hadn't been far off the size of my stump, and it had reduced me to tears as it went in. Now I was sweating buckets as Dr Tavakkoli rubbed a cotton bud on the back of my leg to see where I was sensitive and drew an X at each point. My leg had about twenty of these drawn on it by the time he finished. Although I now had a socket that didn't put any pressure on this part of my leg, the actual skin and nerves themselves were still really sensitive and uncomfortable. He applied some numbing cream and I had to wait with Natalie for half an hour for it to settle in. I was dreading it, as even the bloody cotton bud hurt! On going back in, it was apparent that the numbing cream may as well have been shaving cream – it hadn't done anything to numb the leg.

He pulled out these needles that looked like they should be used to tranquilise horses and definitely not going anywhere near the back of my leg. My stump had next to no muscle – it was skin, sciatic nerve and bone – and these needles, all three of them, looked long enough to go right through to the other side. Here I was, an ex-infantry soldier, I'd been shot and pulled trucks and thrown 100kg stones around like marbles, yet this was up there with the circumcision in terms of panic! The first one went in and it was like a scene from The Exorcist. I let out every swear word known to man and had another nineteen injections to go. I could feel tears rolling down my face, even though I knew a camera for the programme was taking in all the action.

Here endeth my dignity!

But if it worked, I'd have a comfortable socket and a numb leg. The possible outcome from having botox was a painless surface area for three months. I'd have three or four more appointments and, hopefully, each time the area that needed injecting would have shrunk in size. As the exorcism concluded and I was passed a tissue to dry my eyes, I apologised to Dr Tavakkoli and his assistant for my colourful language, slipped my leg on and made my way out to Natalie.

An interview as a couple was the last item of the day for us and then we could head home. As we sat there, both of us thanking everyone for this opportunity, I could feel the leg going cold and numb, and by the time we got back home, I couldn't feel it at all. It was the perfect outcome. In my interview, I said that to leave there with no feeling at all would be amazing, and so it was. I was extremely grateful.

In total, I continued visiting Pat for six months and I owe her a great deal – she changed my outlook on life. I also owe the prosthetists at Poldark a huge debt of gratitude and the people involved with the Dr Christian programme for contacting me in the first place. With a much more settled leg and a much calmer, more optimistic mind, I was hopeful that 2019 would be a far better year.

16

ENJOYING THE MOMENT

With the ongoing botox injections in Harley Street and my new socket fitting comfortably, 2019 was looking to the better year I'd hoped for. I travelled down to see Dr Tavakkoli at his Harley Street centre every few months, and each time the pain of the procedure was just as horrible. But it was a pain I just had to grin and bear, because the results were brilliant. Each time I travelled down, I'd be sweating profusely as I exited the underground station, knowing how much the injections hurt. But the previous few months outweighed the five minutes of pain. The injections helped to completely numb the leg, better than anything I could have hoped for. Each time I saw Dr Tavakkoli, the area that needed botox injections reduced until, eventually, they'd done their job in hugely reducing the hypersensitivity in my skin and also desensitizing the sciatic nerve.

Following each appointment, I knew I'd bought myself another few months of virtually pain-free walking, and that was an investment worth making. It allowed me to walk to pick my children up from school – something I hadn't been able to do for so long. There was a time when the headteacher at their school allowed me to park in the staff car park right next to the entrance. It was clear to see I could barely put one foot in front of the other. Now I was able to walk steadily uphill for a good ten minutes, faster and more comfortably. I certainly felt happier and, being able to draw a line under counselling, I no longer felt the need to look back. It was time to set goals and look forward. The next step would be amputee football. What had begun as something to get me socialising, through walking football, had inevitably grown into the curiosity of wanting to play properly as an amputee. This was football played on crutches, minus the prosthetic leg, in teams of seven, with the goalkeeper missing an arm. I felt mentally ready to be a part of a team and wanted to recapture the nervous tension of sitting in a changing room before a game.

I was given that chance by Peterborough United's amputee football team. Their opening league fixtures were to be held in London against Arsenal Amputees and Brighton and Hove Albion Amputees. I hadn't had the chance to meet any of the players before the day and, to be honest, I was mainly travelling down to learn a bit about the game, to watch people's techniques, and to take away something that I could work on. But a shortage of available players meant I was thrown in at the deep end, and it really was a deep end!

It was a quiet changing room. The lads were mainly late teens to early twenties and here I was, sporting a power belly and a bald patch. I mean, a couple of the players weren't even born when I joined the army – that really made me feel old! What I lacked in technical ability, I hoped I could make up for in leadership. It was years since I'd been in a changing room before a match, and the last time was playing for the Grenadier Guards in the polar opposite of changing rooms. Those blokes were all very vocal and mid-to-late twenties, so this felt very different.

We made our way out to warm up, and it was evident that what these Peterborough lads lacked in conversation, they more than made up for in ability. It was an eye-opener from their first touches to their finishing and their turn of pace. I noticed early on that their crutches were all taped at the cuffs, which was to prevent their forearms slipping out, as I'd find out soon. Many of their crutches were short in length, and so mine stood out as being too long – again, that was clearly something their experience had taught them. This was their area of expertise, and I was keen to learn.

The game against Arsenal started and I felt out of my depth from the kick – I'm sure some players would say that I'm still out of my depth now. I was a presence on the pitch, but not for my movement or technical ability, but my size – I was still very much built like a Strongman and the pre-match team photograph highlighted that. We were a man down before we even kicked off. Then, following an injury to one of our players, we were down to five against Arsenal's seven in the first half. It was pouring down, so I was a little nervous that I'd slip on the crutches. There's an added vulnerability to playing on crutches – it's not having that protected feeling of a carbon fibre socket to keep your stump intact if you fall. These players were clearly past worrying about that; their tackling was as aggressive and committed as in the able-bodied game. I felt comfortable with opposition players backing up into me, as I had my power belly for them to turn and get around, but facing players one on one felt like I was just watching them go past me. The pace of some of these lads was phenomenal, and I spent a large part of that game just in awe at the ability levels.

As a defender, it was a nightmare game to start in and could have been really disheartening, with Arsenal camped in our half for what seemed like the entirety of the game. Instead, I was loving it. It was something I'd really missed – being part of a team. Strongman had turned sour and, aside from the close friends I'd made, I felt more and more isolated. This was different: we were losing, but together. There was no finger pointing or excuses or blame, just hard-working lads battling until the end of the game.

I could feel my back cramping up, but it was pain I could use as a motivator. I now knew the level of the league and the players I was alongside and up against, so I knew I needed to put in a lot of time to improve. I'd have to get better sharpish, with the fixture against

Brighton coming straight after. I'd gone from competing at the top of two sports, bodybuilding and Strongman, to quickly realising I was at the bottom of this sport and, strangely, I liked that. It was a different pressure – pressure to improve, not for myself, but for the benefit of these talented lads.

Peterborough's pitch was as quiet as the changing rooms and instinct took over me as I grew into the game. I'd been involved in the game in some capacity for over twenty years, so I still had a tactical understanding of football, and I wanted to try and bring out the confidence in these lads with encouragement. Not knowing me and me being the new player, they may well have taken it as patronising, but that passion and aggression in me made its way to the surface.

The Brighton game was a rough one. I had my work cut out from the off with their forward, who I've since enjoyed a few feisty battles with, but he was a handful that day – elbows, head butts, studs to my one and only foot, constantly talking in my ear about how bad I was. I loved every second of it and, despite starting the match without a full team, we battled to a 1-1 draw. The changing room was a sombre one, but I drew heart from the fact that we'd just battled with a depleted team and me at the back, who was completely new to this. It felt like, with a full squad, we had the makings of something. After raining all day, I returned to my car, only for the downpour to stop almost as soon as I got in. Results aside, I had plenty to work on and, unlike in my starts to life in bodybuilding and Strongman, it didn't begin with a win, so it could only get better – and I was determined that I would too.

I was still spending a lot of time on my prosthetic leg; I was comfortable on it and enjoyed the independence it gave me. But football provided me with more than being a part of a team and getting back to playing my favourite game, it showed me just what could be done on crutches. Many of these players didn't have the luxury of a prosthetic leg, and so used crutches every day to get about – and did it with ease. That's how it looked from the outside, anyway. Spending time with them was beginning to alter my mindset of needing to be on my leg all the time, and some of the advice I received in London was to spend more time off it. I took it on board, taped up my cuffs, just like they all did, and started going out of the house on crutches by choice – something I was reluctant to do before meeting these lads. I started cooking meals at home on crutches, to grow my confidence on them and to build up my balance, as I was now training with three separate walking football clubs every week.

I always had the attitude that I had to be the hardest worker. I knew I was lightyears behind the ability of some of these lads, and maybe they didn't rate me highly in comparison to what they could do, but they'd see that I was more than willing to put in the effort. Many of them had either been born missing limbs or lost them at a young age, mostly to cancer. Veterans were quite open in talking about how they lost a limb or two, but some of these lads were a bit more reserved about it. I felt a sense of gratitude that, although school wasn't great for me, I was able to experience childhood with two legs and I was able to join the army. Having got to know some of these players, I could honestly say that most of them would have made great soldiers. They were all resilient, and I found out that they played football like this at school. I'd been playing football on crutches for less than six months and some of these lads had been playing that way from the age of six.

Meeting so many people with disabilities in bodybuilding, Strongman and football, and also the other veterans I knew who'd gone on to do amazing things, really gave me new perspectives. I learned a lot about the human mind and the ability of people to take setbacks on the chin, process them and go again. They've all been valuable life lessons – lessons that are important for me to pass on to my own children. I'd like them to have that resilience and determination, but also an appreciation of all they're lucky to have. Sport has been an anti-depressant for much of my time as an amputee, it's a shot of "stop feeling sorry for yourself," and it provided a way to look at this disability, not negatively, but as a blessing. That may sound strange; I'm missing a leg, how can that be a good thing?

But I've learned so much about others, their struggles, their mental toughness, and that many with disabilities are a damn sight better at sport than some able-bodied people I've crossed paths with! The six years I've had in disability sport have taken me to places and made me do things I never would have done had I not lost my leg. There's no way my Company Sergeant-Major would have let me disappear to eat a meal every three hours or to practice pulling trucks or to fly off to America or be interviewed for television. I'm glad I had all those surreal experiences. Hindsight is a wonderful thing, but I wish I'd had the thought processes I have now, and my determination and maturity, when I was in the army and in secondary school. I look back and think I'd have made a better soldier to have had these experiences and to have spent time in the company of some of these people with disabilities before I lost a leg.

On reflection, I also think that, with a clear head and without the burning hurt and pain I was carrying inside for so long, I would have maybe settled into Strongman better and left a different impression on people. Reflecting on that, and the way in which I came away from the sport, led me to tell Natalie that I wanted to do one more Strongman competition, to be able to leave the sport on happier terms, to enjoy the whole day. I wanted to finish in America – the lads there weren't just some of the best disabled strongmen in the world, but some of the nicest. As I sat there at the "Arnolds" in 2018, it was the American lads who welcomed me over and involved me, and that didn't go unnoticed.

So, after convincing Natalie that ending on a high was something I wanted to do, I entered America's Strongest Disabled Man again. I wanted to show them what a healthy, happy me was like to be around – something people in Strongman hadn't seen much of. Now, I had the dilemma of not just wanting to improve on the football pitch, but also of doing myself justice in America.

The difference this time, though, was that I didn't place any pressure on myself about where I wanted to finish. I just wanted to have fun, and it actually made my training so much more enjoyable. I didn't go mad with my eating, I just prepared to compete with a smile on my face and I had that same approach to football. I'd competed with self-imposed pressure for the past few years and, in a strange way, I was enjoying not being anywhere near the top. I was just happy to be in the moment.

The football season, with a full squad, went from strength to strength. We were missing our England players for those first two matches I'd been involved in and it was clear, once they came back to the side, just why they were international players. The skill and freedom they brought to the team sent us on a run that saw us finish top of the Southern League and progress to the National League play-offs.

I was growing in confidence every time we met up, and the international players were slightly older and more vocal, so it really did feel like the days of having two legs. Sometimes that "two legs" confidence would get me carried away and I'd end up on my backside, looking up, as life reminded me that there were some things I definitely still couldn't do on crutches. I'd been so used to walking at a relatively slow pace on my prosthetic that I was loving moving quick enough to actually feel that cold, burning lung sensation I missed.

One player who wasn't at the first fixture, but was available for the rest of the season, was Ben Houghton and I know he'll be reading this, so now is my chance to sing his praises. Of all the players I've played alongside and against in my short time in amputee football, he is by far this country's most talented player. The man can do things with a football that I rarely saw in the able-bodied game. His first touch is phenomenal and his ability to finish from anywhere on the pitch is second to none. This is a man who has scored in amputee World Cups against some of the best players in the world, and it's easy to see why. I genuinely believe that, had Ben grown up with two legs, he would have, without doubt, made it as a professional footballer. Yet, for someone of such talent, he's one of the most down to earth and humble players in the league, who isn't afraid to put the team first and get stuck into the dirty work. We are of similar age and outlook and have the same sense of changing room humour, so we clicked straight away. Since getting to know each other, he's the one player to have happily taken time out to help me and others improve. Using his experience to assist us is something he didn't have to do, so it says a lot about the man.

Having such a work ethic throughout the team is what shaped our season. There were others that had great individuals, teams whose heads you could get inside and teams that played some beautiful football. What separated us was our work rate – every man put in maximum effort from start to finish. We were very much the Rocky Balboa of the league, the resilient underdog. This was the impression we left throughout the season – and on one hot March weekend in Birmingham.

The League Cup was a coming together of all eight English teams and Partick Thistle of Scotland. We had to play each six-man team in ten-minute matches. Manchester City and Everton arrived in club minibuses, full tracksuits and enough players to field three separate teams. Not many people gave us much of a chance, but our plan for the day was to leave with our heads held high. We set up much like a Jose Mourinho team, getting amongst the opposition. It wasn't pretty, but it certainly proved effective, as we went on to only concede one goal in the eight matches. It was exhausting, yet one of my proudest days on a football pitch, as we held on and held on, literally throwing ourselves in the way of anything and everything. With my lack of pace and in the middle of preparing to go to America to compete, I was the last man at the back, just talking constantly to the younger lads and organising us as best I could. To come away from that tournament a player short and only conceding one goal in the final minute of our last game when tiredness had crept in, was to me, as a defender, as satisfying as scoring a hat-trick!

May came around and it was time to switch sporting priorities and fly to Columbus, Ohio. One of the lads I met at the "Arnolds" kindly offered to put me up in his place for the week – James Spurgin, someone I hold in equally high regard as Ben Houghton. James was run over while on his motorbike in the States, and the severity of the nerve damage meant that his arm was of no use and just hung next to his body. The muscle wastage, especially next to the Strongman frame that James has, made his dead arm obvious. Yet I've seen that man do unthinkably strong things – lifting an atlas stone from the floor to overhead, deadlifting and overhead pressing. There is honestly nothing he isn't strong at, and being around people like James is exactly what I alluded to earlier – it's infectious, to surround yourself with such amazingly strong people, mentally as well as physically.

I flew over having trained hard, and it was the most relaxed I'd felt leading up to a competition. I knew it was the last time I'd compete in Strongman and I was going to savour all five events and the company of people I respected and admired in equal measure. When competing in America, I always preferred to fly over a few days early to adjust to the time difference and enjoy just about every restaurant Columbus had to offer. The day before competing, we ate at four different restaurants and I comfortably consumed around twelve thousand calories. I was itching to compete; it was like filling a car with rocket fuel instead of diesel.

It was nice to see some familiar faces on the day of the competition. The new ones, like most Americans on hearing my accent, thought I was Australian. I always respected the American athletes for how much they encouraged each other, it was a great atmosphere to be part of and I felt it was something the sport was lacking in England. Pats on the back, well wishes and genuine messages of good luck were given to each strongman as they stepped up to take centre stage for each event. All round, it was a relaxed, friendly, yet still competitive competition, and I genuinely think if "Britains" was held to the same level of sportsmanship as that day in Ohio, I'd have stayed in Strongman. I even had the privilege of talking to one wheelchair-bound athlete who'd been a police officer during the terrorist attacks in New York on 9/11, and I felt such respect for him. He'd contracted an illness from the debris and smoke that affected his nervous system and resulted in him ending up in a wheelchair. I could have skipped the competition and listened to him all day.

I loved the sport and I loved pushing my body to the absolute limit, and America was renowned for being a genuinely heavy competition, which appealed to me. It started with a 120kg Viking press. Sat in a wheelchair, limiting any back support and putting all the load on the shoulders, it was as many repetitions as possible in one minute. I managed thirteen and was delighted with how far I'd come from the "Worlds" in 2016, failing to press a 90kg log once. Pressing 120kg 13 times, regardless of competing, showed how far I'd come, although the lack of back support and the cold and rain made me look like an old man as I limped out of the wheelchair.

I went on to win the next event, the prone row, something I hadn't done before. It relied on back strength, so I knew I could do well. I trained for it in Atlas and, thankfully, it was a similar set up. Three lifts each and the maximum lift wins. It was a tactical event, people calling each other's bluff as to whether they were going to attempt that weight, but then skipping it to attempt the next weight. It was all in good fun and, after my first lift felt really comfortable, I held back and held back until there were two of us and won the event with a 525lb lift. It was nice to do a different type of event, as the ones in "Britains" were pretty much the same five or six every year.

We then made our way inside as the weather took its toll, and it was on to the Crucifix Hold – a nemesis of mine. I made light of it and walked up laughing and joking and mocking myself for the fact that it would probably take longer to strap me in than the time I would manage to hold up the two hammers. But I surprised myself, finishing fourth and passing a minute. I was glad that that event was done and I would never have to do it ever again!

I was beginning to wish I'd had this same clear head all through my Strongman career. I'd gone from taking myself to deep, dark places in my head and struggling to calm down afterwards, to laughing as I approached an event that I knew I stood absolutely no chance of winning. Maybe Strongman would have been better for me on an emotional level if I'd been in the middle of the pack and focused on enjoying the day, rather than being so driven to win and using events as opportunities to vent my upset.

The fourth event was a maximum sandbag load. Sat in a wheelchair, wedged between two oil barrels, with a sandbag on one to be lifted much like an atlas stone and thrown onto the opposite barrel, while letting go in between each repetition. There were three weights to choose from and we could pause the time to opt to increase the weight, but not go down in weight. Fewer reps on the heaviest sandbag would outscore many reps on the lightest sandbag, so again, it was a mind game. The sandbags were 225lb, 275lb and 300lb, but they had been sat in the rain all morning, so they were wet and heavier than they were supposed to be.

As the event went on, blokes became more confident in attempting the 300lb bag and I was no different, laughing as I said I'd give it a go. The weight and size of the sandbag smothered my head as, unlike an atlas stone, the bag took to being a dead weight on my shoulder, my neck and my head, and twisting was even harder, especially in a wheelchair. Yet I loved it – it was a proper test of strength. These were World's Strongest Man weights, and I was going to go all out. I managed two full reps with the 300lb bag and took second place, feeling like I'd just finished an appointment with a chiropractor.

I was hoping our last event was going to go ahead – pulling an American truck outside. But the weather dictated that the event was inside, and we'd instead be pulling a weighted sled. This was to be my last event in Strongman, and it was one of my best. I really enjoyed the day and it felt like the perfect way to finish. That perfect way to end went even better, as I won the sled pull and finished in the sport as I'd started, winning a pulling event.

I finished the competition in second place and actually did well enough to qualify for the World's Strongest Disabled Man again, but I was just pleased to have won two events and finished as high as I did when I looked around to see the standard of people I'd just competed with. Unlike the "Arnolds", the day was finished with us all making our way together across the road for Mexican food and beers. I thanked Chris, the organiser, for allowing me the chance to compete in his tournament. I thanked every athlete for their support, not just on that day, but throughout Strongman, and hoped I'd shown them a glimpse of what I was like to be around when I was in a good place. Then it was back to England, and now I could concentrate solely on football and losing this weight.

Upon my return, I had a month to prepare for the National League title play-offs – the top two teams from the south and the top two teams from the north. It couldn't get any bigger in terms of amputee football. Again, we were the underdogs and drew Everton in the semi-finals, who had a wealth of experience: a big squad, the majority of which were involved with England, either in the past or currently. I was loving football, and the only downside to the amputee league was that the fixtures were only once a month and not every week. But it meant that, when I stepped on the pitch, I gave absolutely everything, like each game was my last. To this day, I still vividly remember my final game on two legs – I never expected that to be the last time I'd play able-bodied football. So I think of that each time I play. Although my body isn't getting any younger, in my mind I'm a teenager again.

Football was my escape as a teenager, as I was mainly surrounded by players that weren't aware of what school was like, and so I always felt at my happiest and my most confident on a football pitch. Twenty years later, I get those very same feelings. I get nerves as well, a lot. In Strongman, it was only myself that I'd let down, but sitting in a changing room with players who give everything, I never want to be the one to perform badly. I was always fully aware I wasn't the best in the team, but I knew my effort and commitment could rub off on others.

The day of the play offs arrived, and I'd managed to start shifting the weight I'd held on to for my competition in America. The normal nerves and four or five trips to the toilet and one or two at the service stations on the journey up were in full swing – followed by a precautionary extra trip on arriving at Sutton Coldfield's ground, the venue for the play-offs.

There was some hanging around, which made it more nerve-wracking, and I had time to sit with Natalie and Dad in one of the stands before kick-off, while my boys enjoyed running up and down the terraces. Walking out against Everton, I was tense, and having my family there almost made me try too hard. It was a hot day, 30°C with no shade by the time we kicked off, which played its part in the tempo of the game. Everton were happy to sit and let us have the ball, waiting to hit us on the counterattack. As the half wore on, chances were building at either end, but our regular season had seen us keep a lot of clean sheets. Then a brilliant long-distance curl from one of the Everton players put us 1-0 down. We were definitely still in the game, though, and levelled shortly after.

As half time came, players from both sides tried to find shade and my dad came over. He hadn't seen me play since I was seventeen and couldn't believe the standard of amputee football. Since that time, football had evolved into getting the ball down and playing; gone were the days of lumping it up field. In all my years growing up playing

Sunday League, I had numerous runners-up medals, but had never won a trophy – always the bridesmaid and never the bride! Now I was clinging onto the hope of reaching the final. That played a big part in my nerves, as it genuinely felt like this team could change my luck – until a minute into the second half and a long ball upfield from Everton saw me slip as the last defender and Everton took the lead again.

I could feel my bottom lip go, as that feeling of letting everyone down came to my mind. After that I avoided the ball for a minute or two, trying to use my age and experience to snap myself out of it. Natalie and Dad could see my head had dropped, but I was determined to put it right and, instead of hiding, put in every ounce of effort I had. But as the game ticked away and our chances were all near misses, that thought of watching someone else lift a trophy was like a black cloud – until, Gary, our forward, stepped up with two late goals and sent us on our way to the final. I'm not sure anyone celebrated as much as me. I was a relieved man, and I turned to the stand where my family were and gave them the biggest of grins.

I apologised to the team for my mistake, but it was in the past. I was still nowhere near the level on my crutches that most of these players were and I felt like I was just a spare part in an otherwise elite level of football. I couldn't wait for the final, where we would, yet again, be the underdogs against Manchester City – a team full of England internationals with lots of pace and lots of goals. We'd seen them pick teams apart throughout the season, but hearing a flippant comment from one of the spectators that it was only a matter of how many we'd lose by fired us all up. It was much like the comment of me not making it in the army from my dad.

Unlike the game against Everton, where we had plenty of the ball, this needed to be a dogged performance, with every player a brick wall, willing to throw themselves in front of everything that would come our way. We could beat Man City, but we would have to beat them as a team. We were confident that would be the difference and would frustrate their top players, which is exactly how the game was panning out. Chris, our goalkeeper, stopped everything and I even cleared two off the line myself. Our forwards were for large parts extra defenders, but our resilience was paying off and our confidence that we could win this began to show. I just sat as a sweeper – I didn't have the pace or the turning circle to keep up with their top players, but I could cover the players who were pressing them and then get my body in the way. Their team started to get frustrated and argue amongst themselves and, once that happened, we were able to see the game out with a 4-2 win!

I seemed to be more emotional than most of the other players. I don't know if it meant more to me or not, but I'd grown up in an era of seeing the likes of Paul Gascoigne and Stuart Pearce shed tears as tough men on the pitch. It was visible how much it meant to those players, and I was no different in showing my joy, but there was a strange feeling afterwards, where I almost felt a little embarrassed for being so happy. I suppose that's more reflective of modern football, where players win a big game and walk off much like any other match. I'd waited well over twenty years to win a trophy in football; winning in bodybuilding and Strongman were different, I didn't have lasting memories of near misses in those as a boy. But football was my life growing up, and having gone from slipping in the game against Everton, to being league champions meant I was filled with feelings of euphoria.

After the presentation of the trophy, I waited patiently for my moment to get to hold it and the first thing I wanted to do was take it over to my boys. My eldest, Ellis, had watched the game, but Ethan much preferred climbing and running around the terraces and was almost oblivious to the fact we'd won. He was ready to go home, and Natalie had to drive, as my back was cramping and the adrenaline had worn off and I was knackered. My head was pounding from playing in the heat, but I smiled almost all of the way. Little did I realise that my efforts throughout the season would be rewarded with being voted player of the year by the other lads in the team.

Strongman had affected how involved I got with things, so I kept myself to myself off the pitch, not wanting to say anything wrong and impact on something I loved, so to earn their recognition in that way meant the world to me. To go from Strongman, where I seemed to be the pantomime villain, to a sport where I was accepted and welcomed almost eclipsed the feeling of winning the league.

Almost.

Following the conclusion of our season, it was time to try to bury the bad memories of Florida and enjoy a holiday in Mexico. I'd felt guilty ever since things started to pick up for me – that it took such an extraordinary holiday for me to come to terms with seeking help. I knew it'd been a raw subject at home, but perhaps if I hadn't hit rock bottom on that holiday, I might have continued to spiral into a depression that was already affecting my marriage and life in general. Opening up certainly gave Natalie some understanding of where I was mentally, and I'd managed to regain her trust that it was okay to go on holiday – something she was understandably dubious about. That holiday marked what felt like a new chapter, just as I finish this one.

So, as I come to the end of writing this chapter and indeed, the book itself, I can finish on what seems the perfect ending to this journey up to now. That is to say that, as I write this, it's just a few days until the ninth anniversary of losing my leg. In those nine years, I've tried and tried to get in contact with each and every person involved in helping to keep me alive. More than anything – more than piecing together the parts that are blank – I just want to thank them. I have so much to be grateful for and so much to live for. But one person I've also wanted to get in touch with since that moment, was the poor bloke on the other end of the weapon that shot me.

I've never held any malice against him. It was an accident, he couldn't see me, he was one side of a wall and I was the other. Accidents happen in the workplace, it just so happens that the consequences of accidents in that workplace were a little more severe than the average. I know he didn't realise I was the other side, and I know it must have played on his mind. Representatives involved higher up in my own regiment and those from the Ministry of Defence never took it any further when, at the end of each interview, I'd ask if I could speak with him. We were from different regiments and I didn't know him, but I worried about him more than I worried about myself. I wondered how he felt, and I just wanted to reassure him that I was okay and that losing a leg, in many ways, has enhanced my life.

Yes, I miss the army and all that comes with it. I enjoyed being away on operational tours, but I also love that I now play an active role in my children's lives, something I might not have done had I still been serving. I see changes in them almost daily, as they grow into two fine young men, changes I'd miss out on if I was five thousand miles away for six months at a time. I was just an expendable number as an infantry soldier, replaced in my role almost in an instant, but I hope the legacy I've been fortunate enough to build up in these past nine years is one my children can be proud of, and I hope that I've set a good example for them to grow into resilient, strong, determined men.

So, in many ways, when I'm walking in comfort and I'm in a gym or on the football pitch or sat reading a story in a funny voice to my boys, my life is better than it would have been if I still had two legs. These are the things I wanted to pass on to that lad.

And as it so happens, as I finish writing, we've just been put in contact after all this time…

EAFA Play-Off Final: Stood with my boys and the league winners' trophy. This feeling was worth waiting over twenty years for!

Peterborough United Amputee Football Team: EAFA League champions 2019

EAFA Super League: Getting the opportunity to be on the pitch with some of the country's best amputee footballers

EAFA End of Season awards: Voted Peterborough United player of the year 2019

Mexico 2019: In a cenote

ACKNOWLEDGEMENTS

Firstly, thank you to each and every one who has shown such support and interest in my new path since my injury. Much of that has come from social media, and the response has been overwhelming from day one. I thought I might get a few blokes from the regiment follow what I'm doing for a little bit, but I never ever expected the reach it would grow to have. I've been inundated with messages of support – messages that have filled my heart with warmth, when people who are facing illnesses and amputations of their own contact me to say that they've found inspiration from my own recovery to face theirs head on and are feeling more positive about their own futures. I've had messages from people to say that they'd been feeling suicidal, but they looked at what I'd been doing and it gave them the motivation to keep going. With what happened to Spence, these are the messages that really hit home and made me want to keep pushing myself and try to help whenever and wherever I could.

We have a roof over our heads, food on the table and smiles on our faces. Through my military pension, we are able to live a happy life, and so, I wanted this book to help others. The proceeds of each copy of this book sold will be going to Aiden's Funds, a charity that we fully support. Aiden was a friend of my children and a pupil in my wife's class who, sadly, lost his life to cancer. He was no older than my youngest, Ethan, is now. Since losing their son, his parents, Rick and Claire, set up the charity to support children going through cancer, by taking in Christmas gifts, Easter eggs, anything to keep them entertained during their time in hospital. All done by just the two of them and a close friend of theirs. This makes me even more grateful for each copy sold, as the money will benefit them greatly. So thank you, I hope you've found it a worthwhile purchase and have enjoyed reading it.

It's been difficult to be so open, but I thought it might give people an idea of why I expend every ounce of effort I have in all that I do. I dread sitting in the changing rooms knowing that much of my private life will be common knowledge to those who read this, knowing friends I served with never knew what sort of time I had at school or the thoughts that entered my head on every painful day I had with my leg before counselling. I hope people who didn't think too highly of me in Strongman understand that I wasn't coping very well behind all of the aggression and competitiveness and that, if we crossed paths now, they would meet a much happier version of me. I actually wish this version of me, this slightly more mature version – only slightly – had been the one to have served. I look back now and realise I was just a big kid in Battalion, which meant I didn't take anything too seriously, but also meant I was a bit of a dick. To go from hating school to feeling like I was a part of a family in the Queen's Company was something I was so, so proud of.

I'd like to give a special mention and a thank you to all of the following:

Every school, gym, workplace, function and club that invited me in to hear my story – the fact you showed such an interest is humbling.

To my wife for sticking with me through every tour, every low, my injury, loving me just the same despite looking noticeably different and for laughing with me almost every single day. My life is about making you and the boys as happy as you make me and repaying you for not leaving my side when I'd lost all hope.

Thank you to the genuine friends I made during my time in Battalion, the ones who sat by my bedside as I wasted away, the ones who picked up the phone and the ones who continue to meet with me to this day.

Thank you to my dad; you have made me the most stubborn,

determined person I could be. Wanting to win your praise and approval has undoubtedly helped me achieve things and to hear, at my passing out parade, at "Britains", the "Arnolds", in the hospital bed in intensive care, that you were proud of me, meant more than you'll ever know.

To Spence, Woody, Dean and all the safety staff and medics who gave me every fighting chance of living and seeing my wife and children again, I will be forever in your debt and you'll always be held in the highest regard in our home.

Thank you to each and every nurse, doctor and surgeon at Medicine Hat, Calgary and the Queen Elizabeth hospitals, for your care and determination to keep me alive. I don't remember much of the early few days, but Natalie tells me that one of the first surgeons to treat me cried when he found out that the operation he performed on me hadn't saved my leg. You are all amazing. As is every single member of staff at Headley Court, who took me from a weak, feeble, underweight man in a wheelchair, to someone determined to push the limits of what could be possible with one leg.

Thank you also to the prosthetists and staff at Luton and Dunstable limb fitting centre, who carried on the great work that Headley Court had done and continue to keep me walking.

Thank you also to all those involved at Poldark Prosthetics in Watford, for providing me with a pillow of a socket at a time when I really didn't know how or when I would walk again. Having that comfort kickstarted me getting my life back on track.

Thank you to all involved at the Doctor Christian's special clinics programme and Doctor Tavakkoli, I may not have seemed that grateful as the botox injections were going in, but they were life changing.

Thank you in particular to Iain Farrell and Matt Ellmer of the Grenadier Guards. You both went above and beyond your roles and are considered family friends. I'm not sure that anyone else could have carried out the roles you both have as well as the two of you.

Thank you to Spider, Bruce, Ed and Danny, who motivated and inspired me with your positive attitude towards your own injuries during our time on ward 412 in hospital. You are all amazing individuals and you absolutely set me on a positive path in my recovery through your own resilience and outlooks.

Thank you to everyone involved at Pagnell Property Maintenance for adapting my home when I didn't have much in the way of independence. In particular, thank you to Phil Benson who, although no longer with us, helped make my house a home and made it so that my wife no longer needed to put her back out helping me in and out of the bath.

Thank you to Lee Thompson of the NPC in Texas for inviting me over to the States to compete, and to Phil Heath for allowing me the honour to stand next to you on stage. It was a surreal experience and one I will never forget.

Thank you to Rob Creighton, who went out of his way to help both myself and the other disabled strongmen in having a place to safely train, for giving up your time to help us all in setting up, packing away and making some great days that I know everyone appreciated and enjoyed, and also for accompanying me in some of the best nights of drinking. Remembrance Days with you and all the other lads have become biblical, and you have no idea how much I look forward to being in the company of you all – although Natalie dreads it, as I'm often a mess for a week after!

One of my biggest thank yous is reserved for Pat, the sweetest and most understanding lady, for listening to me at my lowest and for piecing together the jigsaw of my emotions and helping me find some positivity – each session helped more than I can say.

My final thank you is for each and every individual that supports me and follows me. Without that support, I'd never have written this. I've had counselling and feel in the best place I've been since losing my leg, and writing this book has been therapeutic in itself.

It's something I'm glad I've done.

Next year marks ten years since I lost my leg and I hope to add many more stories and memories to what has already been an amazing second chance at life. I had regrets as I lay in that hospital bed, hoping I'd get the chance to be a good dad and husband and to tick things off my bucket list. If I'm ever in that position again, I'll have no regrets!

A man amongst giants. Stood with fellow local Grenadier Guards at our yearly get-together, before we drink ourselves into a state and disappoint our wives!

I'm very fortunate to have a great family on Natalie's side, who welcomed me into theirs from the moment we met

I love these three to pieces. My brothers-in-law: Rob, James and Matt

London in the sky: Enjoying a three-course meal, elevated above the 02 arena on a crane!

With Natalie at the Shard in London

IN MEMORIAM

The term "legend" is thrown around all too freely, but you are a legend to me and I miss you every day. I don't have many heroes, but this is one –

Spencer Christian Beynon
23 April 1973–14 June 2016

Spencer Christian Beynon, Sgt, 1 Royal Welsh

Printed in Great Britain
by Amazon

61307406R00132